A Canterbury Childhood

A Canterbury Childhood

Scenes of Life in a Small City Between the Wars

KENNETH PINNOCK

ROBERT HALE · LONDON

© Kenneth Pinnock 2009
First published in Great Britain 2009

ISBN 978-0-7090-8773-1

Robert Hale Limited
Clerkenwell House
Clerkenwell Green
London EC1R 0HT

www.halebooks.com

The right of Kenneth Pinnock to be identified as
author of this work has been asserted by him
in accordance with the Copyright, Designs and
Patents Act 1988

A catalogue record for this book is available from the British Library

2 4 6 8 10 9 7 5 3 1

Typeset by e-type, Liverpool
Printed in Great Britain by
the MPG Books Group, Bodmin and King's Lynn

Contents

List of Illustrations

Acknowledgements

My father died shortly after the manuscript of *A Canterbury Childhood* was submitted for publication. He left me with careful instructions for the completion of his selection of illustrations, and for his acknowledgements of those who gave generous help. It has given me great pleasure to play my small role in the completion of his work. I should like to join him in thanking Sidney Santer, Derek Butler, Colin Graham, the Oatenhill Press, the *Daily Mirror*, Kent Libraries and Archive, and Canterbury Library Local Studies Collection for help with illustrations and also Bill Charlton, Debbie Gill, Nick Perren, John Murray, Liz Ward and Victoria Lyle.

Trevor Pinnock

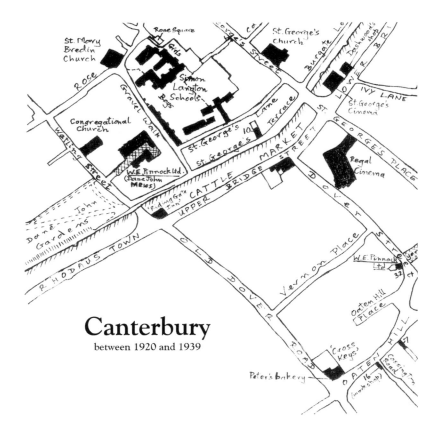

Canterbury

between 1920 and 1939

Preface

WHAT SORT OF a book is this? 'Autobiography' is the obvious answer, but this is one in which the central character stands in the wings as prompter, with no desire to be the actor centre-stage. Some may be tempted to call it history, because it is about a time so long ago that soon it will be beyond living memory. But that would be a mistake, for history demands a rigour and breadth to which I make no claim.

I see it as simply the story, drawn from memory though fortified by much delving into local newspapers, of how I came to explore and, within limits, to understand the forty-acre plot that was my birthright. It tells of a society which flourished here three generations ago and has vanished almost without trace. It is all seen through the eyes of a growing child – myself, so it is a worm's eye view. Yet as I wrote, I was struck again and again by how much was revealed from that humble viewpoint.

Kenneth Pinnock

1

The House of Light and Dark

FOR A LONG while after the great air raid of June 1942, the house on St George's Terrace in which I was born stood gaunt and desolate, ravaged by fire bombs and high explosive, its window frames gaping, its roof open to the sky. Then it was torn down, with its equally forlorn neighbours, to make way for a bus station. The front wall of the Terrace, forming the backcloth to the cattle market, was re-faced in flint and provided with a bastion to match the genuine ones in other parts of the city walls; and a tablet was put up that said – ambiguously or even mendaciously – that the city wall had here been 'restored' in 1952. No one argued that the handsome Georgian terrace itself should be restored or rebuilt. The Festival of Britain was just behind us, and the New Elizabethan Age just ahead: this was a time of new beginnings with scant regard for any virtues of the past. So St George's Terrace passed into history, becoming merely a name without any addresses. Its fine wrought-iron railings went for scrap, and even the pretty 'Gothic' cast-iron drinking fountain, with a chained cup of burnished copper which I was forbidden to use for fear of 'germs', was suddenly whisked away without a word of explanation after standing sentry at the foot of the Terrace since Victorian times.

Here was my home for the first ten years of my life. Even then it was under the shadow of dissolution. On the top floor, the room that my brother and I shared was the only one that was furnished. By the light of the solitary 'bat's wing' flame on the landing, as we went to bed we would see through the half-open doors of the other rooms plentiful evidence of my father's compassion for unwanted lots at auction sales – a tea-chest of sponges (real, not rubber), or trays of perfume bottles, all sickly of scent but fantastically various in their shapes and names and, amid these, relics were scattered strategically to catch the drips from the ceilings. In the basement, which was below ground at the front of the house but not at the back, there were similar signs of decay and neglect. The window of our living room, which we called 'the kitchen' on account of its presumed function, was below the level of the Terrace and rarely visited by the sun, but there was some compensating interest from the trousered or gaitered legs that flashed past it as tradesmen went up and down the steps of the 'area' just outside. At one end of its usually gas-lit interior there was a china-laden dresser, and at the other a small 'kitchener' stove that warmed – but could no longer cook.

Although we didn't know it, this room had been cut out of the 'berm', the huge bank of earth that was piled up in Roman times as backing for their flint wall round the city. Behind it was the scullery, draughty and cold, with yet another kitchener stove, this one almost as clapped-out as its smaller sister. Thanks to its feebleness, our Christmas dinner did not start until the old-fashioned time of 4 o'clock in the afternoon. Unplastered walls, a shallow stone sink, a tap but no hot water system, an uneven brick floor, and a view of a dank little north-facing garden flanked by the sheds for wood and coal, and containing an outside WC which was clearly designed for the servants because it had a seat of bare wood, with no trace of stain or varnish – these were the scullery's depressing features. Yet it had a redeeming virtue – our toy cupboard, from which I could extract my tinplate model of Sir Henry Segrave's record-breaking car, the Golden Arrow, a fifteen-shilling Christmas treat which, once wound up, would rumble over the bricks at nothing like Sir Henry's speed, but fast enough to banish all other thoughts belonging to that part of the house, from Monday's washday steam and scrubbing, or Tuesday's mince (positively the last appearance of the weekend joint), through to the aroma of the new joint on Saturday which marked the beginning of another week's familiar routine.

I remember that house as a place of contrasts – of light and dark, of sound and silence. The front, with the exception of the basement kitchen, blazed with the day's brilliance and resounded to the fascinating clamour of the cattle markets that took place once or twice a week beyond and below the railings of the Terrace. The back had an altogether different character: gloomy and introverted, for its windows looked out on to a sorry little garden terminating in a wall with a gate leading to a dank passage that tunnelled through the blank back walls of a row of cottages fronting on St George's Lane. Over this barricade of brick came some sounds of life, the clang of the shoesmiths' forge and the rhythmic clatter of Mr Jennings's printing works which faced it; and then from time to time there was a sudden upsurge of muffled shouting, dying suddenly as a bell was rung, coming from behind the lichened wall that formed the boundary of the Simon Langton Boys' School. But the day began with bells, first the musical handbell of the muffin man, whose wares I imagined but never tasted, for I saw only in imagination his white-aproned figure with a chef's hat and his tray of warm muffins enfolded in layers of napkins. And soon afterwards there was the massive monotone of Bell Harry (a little hoarse, for he was yet to be re-founded) dinning in the message, 'A quarter past seven, time to get up.' He spoke again at the end of the day, and I heard him then in the unnatural gloom of wartime blackout, with blinds drawn that were thick and dark, though now speckled through age with tiny stars of daylight. But now the words were different, 'A quarter to eight, time for bed.'

To a great extent, the front was the public face not merely of our home but of our entire existence. All our non-tradesman callers came that way. One of the 'regulars' was a little old lady who rattled off a biblical verse as soon as the door was opened, and followed up by delving in a large bag to fish out a printed text and hand it over. The whole operation took seconds rather than minutes. A rather less frequent visitor was Miss Sims. My father told us that she was a stamp collector, and something he added somehow conveyed the fact that she was very rich, and that she financed her hobby partly by acts of meanness. So it proved, for my brother Ron and I observed that on every visit she made a bee-line for the lavatory at the top of the house, not always remembering to flush it as she left.

But the great majority of our callers were the tradesmen who came down to our humble everyday level. Although the Terrace had both a footpath by the railings and a vestigial roadway, there was virtually no vehicular traffic. The milkman arrived pushing a three-wheeled 'float' bearing a great churn, from which he filled brass-mounted cans of polished steel, so that he could ladle our pint or quart into our own jugs. Our baker, Mr Shrubsole, used a similar technique: he pushed an immense two-wheeled cart, with gently swelling sides that made it look like a piece of Buhl furniture, up the slope of the Terrace from St George's Street, and from its pregnant interior he would fill a large basket to carry on his arm as he descended the area steps. We very rarely had anything but one of his delicious cottage loaves, shaped in profile like a figure eight and consisting of a large round lump surmounted by a smaller one – two loaves in one, in fact, for invariably the smaller lump was detached and eaten before the larger one. The large basket did, however, enable my mother to pick a loaf of just the right degree of crustiness, which she promptly dropped into our capacious 'crock' of glazed earthenware with a wooden lid, to be eaten the next day. Alas, Mr Shrubsole's bread was unbelievably good when it was still warm from the faggot-fired oven in Northgate, but new bread was 'indigestible', my mother said, so it had to wait a day before the first of its slices – every one different in size and shape – was cut.

Was there perhaps some likeness between my mother's attitude to bread and the way my parents used their house – a Puritanical shunning of pleasure in favour of alternatives less likely to damage digestion or deplete the purse? Why did we inhabit the basement

Ken used to aim his Golden Arrow toy at the mouse holes in the basement of the house on St George's Terrace

when we could have moved up to Terrace level, using the bright, well-proportioned front room, making a new kitchen in the room behind it, and leaving the basement as a playground for spiders and beetles – and even for the mice whose holes were convenient targets for my Golden Arrow? I can only guess at the answers to these never-asked questions. A new kitchen would have meant a new stove – hence, new building work, a doubtful investment in a rented house. As a coal merchant, my father would never think of installing one of those dangerous, messy gas stoves. And … but it would be tedious to go on about such details. The all-important fact was that Number Ten was rented by my father at ten shillings a week, and why improve a rented house?

But as to the room by the front door, I am baffled. In my recollection, it was never furnished, despite its good proportions and sunny aspect, but served merely to house my pushchair and the discarded wooden crying-enclosure that was incongruously called a 'play-pen'. But a dim memory suggests the possible answer. I recall seeing 'men from the Corporation' making long strips of newspaper, soaking them in what I thought to be – and perhaps was – vinegar and sticking them all round that room's door frame. My brother had been sleeping there when he was found to have diphtheria. The 'fever cart', one of my father's horse-drawn vehicles kept solely for such a purpose, had taken him off to the isolation hospital, and then these men had come to fumigate the room and for a while seal it off. For my mother, the anxiety of that time was perhaps so great, and the recollection of it so painful, that she could never bring herself to use it again.

So, one day we would move: gradually that fact dawned on me, although it didn't actually happen until I was eleven years old. We would become part of that draining-away of population from the centre to the suburbs which had been going on for many years, a process that is written in ripples of change in architectural styles as you move out from the centre, and in a good many novels – such as Arnold Bennett's 'Clayhanger' series.

Yet in the 1930s, there were still a number of tradesmen who lived 'over the shop' in central Canterbury. At the far end of the Terrace, for instance, the veterinary surgeon Mr George Dunkin had a fine detached Regency house, with shrubbery and railings at the front and a good garden at the back, behind which was a yard surrounded by stables, with always-open double doors leading on to Gravel Walk through which his four-footed patients arrived for treatment. Nothing could have been more convenient for both the vet and his clients. Mr Pollard, the jeweller, and his family occupied an old and beautifully timbered first-floor house above his shop in St George's Street, with Woolworths selling a very different class of goods next door and Marlowe's birthplace only a few yards away. And almost opposite Pollard's, my schoolfellow Irene Ward lived with her family in a jettied house so ancient that you stepped down from the pavement to the medieval level, to enter a cavern whose air was always heavy with the scent of the hand-made chocolates that were created somewhere behind the glazed door leading to the parlour.

But increasingly the shopkeepers who could afford it, especially those not tied to their premises by the demands of security or production, were migrating to the southern heights well outside the city wall. This, I believe, was not merely a matter of fashion, of people following a beaten path. Until quite recently in history, even small cities must have had a powerful and sometimes filthy smell. Open sewers were no longer to be found in Canterbury, but there were plenty of horse-manure heaps such as the one at the rear of my father's Mews, and if the breweries were closing one by one, those remaining could still make their presence smelt. From time to time, the tannery spread a pall of nausea over Stour Street and beyond, while residents in the area of King Street had to endure all day the rasping sound of a timber merchant's circular saw. It was no accident that slums and poverty clustered around these industries, and that sometimes in these parts of the city old houses of real quality should fall on hard times.

Living on the Terrace I found literally the ground of my existence, an urban environment that provided rich and even thrilling experiences as I explored it in widening circles, leading in time to a sense that through every chink and crevice of the apparently unchanging fabric of the city was running an immensely strong tide of change, capable in time of utterly transforming it. The battle of new against old was most immediately visible in the decay – but by no means the death, as yet – of horse-drawn transport, for which any temptation to grieve was utterly overwhelmed by excitement at the triumph of the motor car. Shops and shopkeeping were one of the principal stages on which I saw the dramas of everyday life enacted: here, too, I began dimly to realize how the scenes were being shifted and the lines rewritten, though never so drastically as in later years. The already massive inroads of the cinema on old-fashioned, home-based and homespun modes of entertainment entered a new phase with the coming of the 'talkies' and then of the super-cinemas, while radio (or 'wireless' as we invariably called it) suddenly and almost miraculously joined forces with the cinema in cracking the crust of customary attitudes and beliefs. Even print, hitherto the only means of public communication, changed its character, as the tabloids discovered new and more appealing ways of getting through to the mass of the population. I could never have formulated these developments, but I hope that later in these pages I shall be able to explain how they infiltrated my mind through childhood experiences such as seeing a crowd, mainly of women, weeping uncontrollably as they emerged from an early 'talkie', and how in time understanding dawned that life was about change.

My starting-point for this voyage of exploration was that nest of nearly defunct technologies, Number Ten, where we lived in the style of many a Victorian family, lit by gas, using coal for all our heating and cooking, eating bread kneaded by hand and baked in a faggot-fired oven. As I write, seventy or eighty years later, the 'Big Dig' is in progress: archaeologists are excavating a huge area from the Terrace back into the city before redevelopment takes place. They are wonderfully knowledgeable about all sorts of things – dating every kind of pottery, from Neolithic times onward, and identifying all sorts of domestic objects from bone combs to belt buckles. But I can't help wondering if they would be baffled on discovering one of the swivelling brass cranks that carried the bell wire from the front door of our house right down to the row of bells mounted on coiled springs in the basement. And again, what would they make of a neatly contrived whistle with a large knob at one end? Would they know that this came from the lower end of one of the speaking tubes, to be sounded by a sharp puff from one of the floors above as a signal to extract the whistle and listen to an order? Are there any houses where such antediluvian communication systems – not merely pre-electronic, but pre-electric – still exist? If there are, no doubt they give delight to the young of the household, as our speaking-tubes did to Ron and me.

Uneasily poised as we were between the Victorian age and its successor, whatever that might be, I learned very early in life to use the term 'Victorian' as one of disparagement, even abuse: art, architecture, morals, dress – almost every aspect of Victorian life seemed indisputably absurd to me. This childish reaction, no doubt caught from adults, I now see as proof of the power that this tremendous era still exerted. When did it end – 1914, 1939, 1945? It's hard to be sure. What I *do* know is that when, in my teenage years and living in a more or less modern house, I looked back to that kitchen in which the hissing gas fought against the gloom, it all seemed to belong to another century, with everything in life moving to the Holmesian tune of clop-clopping hooves unadulterated by any noise of gear changes. And when I peered at the engravings in Dickens's novels, I felt on familiar ground: those interiors seemed so like the one I had inhabited, and memory even

Taken around 1900, this photograph shows Sarah Pinnock (Ken's grandmother) with her three sons, Walter (Ken's father, on the right), Christopher (centre) and George, together with her widowed daughter, Louisa (right) and Agnes (Christopher's wife)

called up Dickensian characters from my early childhood. There was, for instance, a nurse who came at times to look after my mother, a Gampish figure with the unlikely name of Bertha Biddlecombe, who delighted my brother and me by her habit of offering us twopence to go and buy her a delicacy that she particularly fancied for her tea – a chocolate 'Hayclair'.

Yet whenever I climbed the narrow kitchen stair to the hall, perhaps to answer the imperious ring of Miss Sims or the text lady, I did so with a keen sense of anticipation. For beyond that door was my first playground, the Terrace, basking in the full light of day. My earliest ambition was to get out there at any opportunity, but especially on market days – which were Saturdays and alternate Mondays. My face pressed against the stout railings that ran along the top of what was left of the city wall, I could see almost from end to end of the market. It began at St George's Gate – no longer a turreted medieval gateway as it had been until it was demolished in 1801, but now merely a crossroads where the 'new' road to Dover, cut at the end of the eighteenth century, met the town's main street. It ended only a little short of the point where the old Roman road from Dover pierced the city wall and continued within under the name of Watling Street. Between these two parallel Dover roads, nearly a quarter of a mile apart, another road wriggled much more deviously through a jumble of jettied houses mingled with nineteenth-century cottages, a cluster of public houses to slake the market's thirst and, for good measure, a tiny oasthouse of the Napoleonic period and a large agricultural engineering works. This was Dover Street, the medieval route from the original Dover Road to St George's Gate.

From the Terrace I loved to see this street foaming at the mouth, full from side to side with sheep being propelled by the high-

St George's Terrace overlooked Canterbury's medieval livestock market and the organized turmoil of the weekly livestock auctions

pitched cries of their drovers of 'Hup' and 'Hi', and by the barking
of attendant dogs, towards the double iron gates of the market
immediately opposite. In recent years a former pupil of St George's
School told me how, as a boy, he regularly used to drive a flock to
market along the road from Littlebourne, four miles away, before
entering his school in the main street by nine o'clock. Some cattle
also came on foot, but already many travelled in motorized trans-
porters, to be led down the inclined tailboards and tethered to
immensely strong steel rails at the St George's end of the market,
where the weighing machine stood with its enormous dial
unveiled in honour of this day.

The middle section of the market, opposite our house, was
given over to sheep. All was prepared for their reception by gangs
of men with great sheaves of ready-cut coarse string tucked into
their waistbelts, who strung together wooden hurdles, each one a
piece of rustic craftsmanship, at top speed to form pens with
gated alleyways leading to the little arenas in which the auctioneers delivered their gabbled orations. Gavel in hand, they stood at
portable desks on which they knocked down lot after lot in rapid
succession to buyers whose bids were barely perceptible to the
unpractised eye – certainly not to mine, even from my excellent
vantage point. Here was drama indeed: the befuddled sheep
forced along predestined paths, the brawny assistants ever alert to
the least sign of uncooperativeness, the auctioneers and their
clerks sallying forth, from offices burrowed into the city wall
beneath my feet, to reach the rostra and spray their intent audiences with a machine-gunfire of bids punctuated by bangs of the
gavel. And if I wanted light relief, I could move right, towards the
Watling Street end of the market, to watch the pigs and poultry, to
see hens pulled squawking from their coops, and to speculate
whether any stray dogs had been shut in the City Pound right at
the end of the market.

For a thousand years and more, markets had been held in this
place. Happily, I had no means of knowing such days were numbered. Only a few decades later the site would give way to road

widening, and the market transferred to the outskirts, then to dwindle and die as the century ended. Much as I enjoyed the bustle of market day in full flow, I also looked forward – with no less anticipation – to its end. Quite suddenly, the market would be clear of livestock and customers, the auctioneers' offices closed, and the hurdle pens dismantled. A small army of workmen, some armed with stiff brooms and others with high-pressure hoses, advanced in military formation to scrub clean every inch of the surface. There was something immensely satisfying about that act of ablution. As I soon learned, to watch others performing hard, physical work is always a fascinating occupation: navvies digging holes with pickaxe and shovel, or workmen with vast boilers of tar to be spread on the roads before they are covered with granite chippings. But nothing could compare with this market-cleaning for efficiency, team work, speed and the dramatic finality of the contrast between the ordure and litter that lay in front of the men's brooms and the clean sweep that they left behind them.

For a time – perhaps a surprisingly short time by present-day standards – the Terrace marked the limits within which I was allowed out of the house on my own. But by the time I was six or seven, at first with my brother and then on my own, I was regularly going into the Dane John – which I could reach without ever having to cross a road – to play with a particular friend who lived there. The Dane John, once an area of waste used as a communal drying ground for washing, a burial ground for malefactors and an archers' shooting-ground, had been splendidly landscaped and planted by one Alderman Simmons at the end of the eighteenth century. A pathway was created along the top of the city wall – here at its original height and complete with turrets – which, as Victorian prints show, became a favourite promenade. In due course a noble avenue of lime trees arose along its main axis, and a great hump of earth, the Mound, which was probably the remains of the earliest Norman castle (or 'Donjon') in Canterbury, was shaped up into a gigantic sugar-loaf and provided with a

The Dane John was landscaped during the eighteenth century and the path along the city wall, leading from St George's Terrace, became a favourite promenade during Victorian times

spiral footpath leading at the summit to a monument commemorating Simmons's generosity.

Framed by dark shrubberies, there were broad lawns in which the Victorians had placed an elegant bandstand and a memorial to the dead of the Boer War whose massive hideousness was redeemed only by some of Eric Gill's early lettercutting. On the far side of the main avenue, beyond the Mound and a fountain, were more lawns, which we children tended to avoid because the municipally tended flowerbeds got in the way of our games. In one corner of this area, more than usually rampant mulberries and other shrubs folded protectively round a memorial to Marlowe presided over by the semi-nude figure of the Muse of Poetry, whom an Edwardian City Council had thought inappropriate to her original position opposite the Cathedral gateway, and therefore moved into bosky seclusion.

Along the entire length of one side of the Dane John, interrupted only by the Mound, there ran a twenty-foot steep bank, the rear of the Roman 'berm'. For some reason that we never fathomed, but

MOAT AND TOWER OF CITY WALL, CANTERBURY

Adjacent to the Dane John, the Memorial Gardens (furnished here with a First World War tank) remained a popular playground during the 1920s and 1930s

learned very early to respect, these sloping surfaces of grass were cared for and protected with a zeal that far exceeded any attention given to the lawns. The care came from detachments of Corporation workers who launched a spring offensive each year with sickles and followed it with a heavy beating with broad-bladed bats, renewing their attacks whenever the grass showed signs of developing into tussocks. The protection was the personal responsibility of the Beadle. In our tender years it took us some time to realize that the Beadle was in fact a member of the human tribe. The main evidence for this supposition was that he lived in a rather nice house at the far end of the main avenue of the Dane John; and in time we learned that, like any ordinary mortal, he even had a name, Mr Horne. Before that he had seemed, with his immaculate blue uniform, his peaked cap, his gleaming buttons, his military gait and sharply waxed gingerish moustache, to be authority itself, a pure principle almost untainted by any human connotations. A single wave of his cane could banish a child from the Dane John for a day, a week, for ever, it seemed; and his favourite stentorian cry of 'Git down awf them banks' struck terror into our hearts, innocent though we were of even contemplating such a crime.

On summer evenings the Dane John was the main pleasure-ground of the city, resounding to music and decked with coloured lights, a place for performances by the Canterbury Silver Band and the Masqueraders concert party; and even for dances, its avenue thronged throughout the season, so that the grass verges were worn away to the bare earth. But for us children it was a playground, to be enjoyed during civilized hours when the world was at work, shared only with the old men who gathered to chat and smoke in a specially built shelter alongside the main avenue and conveniently placed opposite a clock whose glass front remained intact year after year. For under the stern eye of the Beadle, hooliganism was nipped in the bud, and vandalism never even began; thus we were left in peace to ride the wooden scooter that my grandfather had made for Ron's use and mine, to bowl an iron hoop that he had also made for me as successor to the wooden one belonging to my learner-driver days, or to try to master the difficult art of whipping a top. Sometimes we got involved in mysterious games played by 'rough boys' with whom we were not supposed to associate and whose plots seemed to consist of an innocent form of gang warfare. But best of all, without doubt, was a game that could only be played in autumn – Houses. We spent hours gathering up leaves and laying them out in lines to form architectural ground-plans. Such a house consisted mainly of a large rectangle divided into smaller rectangles to represent the living room, kitchen and a couple of bedrooms. It seemed that all our houses were in fact bungalows. No doors, internal or external, were shown, but why worry about that when you could move from room to room simply by stepping over the leaf-walls? How this game originated, and whether or not it was purely a local invention, I have no idea; but many a domestic drama was played out within this insubstantial scenery – so often swept away by the park-keepers' besoms, and so easily renewed after each night's downfall of new materials.

Playing in these ways, we had the illusion of being free from parental intrusion, and almost free of parental control, even though our ages ranged from about five to ten. No doubt some of us came from the stucco-fronted early Victorian houses fronting on the Dane John, so that from time to time a mother could see us from her front window. But in later years I realized what a crucial role the Beadle must have played in keeping the Dane John safe and orderly by his presence, usually in person and always in our minds. When I was nine or ten I saw him for the first and only time in action against one of our elders. A tall, personable man in early middle age had rounded up a group of boys and started to instruct them in various kinds of physical exercise, but soon he was under interrogation by the Beadle. The man said he wanted to build up the youth of the nation, to give these boys pride in being British, to show them how to defend themselves … and so on. The Beadle did not argue with him; he listened with silent contempt, then pointed imperiously with his cane towards the gateway, and the man meekly slunk off. The unostentatious but persistent pressure of a man in authority – this, far more than the long list of prohibitions set out in signwriters' fat italics at each end of the avenue – was what guaranteed the peace and order of our hours of play.

Is it romantic nostalgia to think that in Canterbury at that time there was peace and order, not only in the Dane John but more generally, of a kind we do not have today and can see little or no prospect of regaining? Two symbols come to mind in relation to this question. One is the parcels truck – a large, two-handled affair of wickerwork mounted on a pair of wheels – which was pushed each week up the main street from the main post office to one of the banks. The pusher was accompanied, as a security measure, by a colleague, since the contents were the entire week's 'takings'. The other is the Dane John's clock, unguarded yet unharmed year after year in the 1930s. It disappeared long ago, having been damaged several times, and of course it will never return. We have lost it, and the Arcady of which it was part.

2
At Miss Pierce's

A LITTLE DOOR sandwiched between two shops in Guildhall Street opened up a new chapter in my life at the age of five. The door is still there, but it no longer bears a brass plate inscribed:

PREPARATORY SCHOOL
Principal: Miss D. Pierce

From this door a steep uncarpeted stairway led to the first floor above the drapery shop occupying the site at the corner of Guildhall and Orange Streets. Once at the top of the stairs, Miss Pierce's pupils went straight through her sitting room to the changing room, where coats came off and outdoor shoes were exchanged for indoor shoes. Then, passing by the open door of Miss Pierce's parlour, its Georgian sash window full to bursting with the beauty of the Cathedral's Bell Harry Tower just outside, you entered the main classroom. This was a spacious room with large plate-glass windows, clear at the top but painted a translucent white below, but otherwise similar to those of the shop on the ground floor. Indeed, this upper room had once been part of the shop, which had evidently found it necessary to reduce its floor area by half, notwithstanding the pride and confidence with which its name on the fascia board, 'Skinners', was converted by semi-circular flourishes above and below into a kind of cartouche.

Like so much else in my childhood, my education in that place owed much to the Victorian era. Soon I was equipped with pencils and copybook, and sitting at the long desks ranged round the perimeter of that oval room I spent long hours making 'pothooks and hangers', the first elements of letter-forms. The tedium of this employment was interrupted by 'playtime', when we children, about thirty in number and aged from five to seven, were allowed the luxuries of milk, biscuits and conversation. We called it 'play-time', but there was no room for games of any but the most sedentary kinds. For physical activity we had to wait until after school, when on certain days there was dancing. Most of our dances were traditional, the sort of thing you see nowadays on TV adaptations of Jane Austen and Thackeray, and our music consisted of the songs we sang as we danced, while Miss Pierce clapped to make sure we kept in time. We also learned the tunes and words as we clustered round the piano in her drawing room. The staff of Skinners must have been able to tell the day of the week by the occasions when the lusty strains of 'Come lasses and lads, get leave of your dads, and away to the maypole hie' came filtering through their ceiling, accompanied by Miss Pierce's confident chords and the even more confident percussion of the foot that was not engaged with the pedal.

Confidence, clarity, certainty – these were the outstanding characteristics of Miss Daisy Pierce. Without such qualities she could hardly have ventured into the extremely competitive arena of private schooling in the city. Directories of the 1920s show what a wide choice was open to any parents willing to find five guineas or so a term to insulate their infant from the hurly-burly and stringent discipline of the state elementary schools. When my parents chose Miss Pierce's school, first for my brother and then for me, I am sure they did not look simply for the cheapest but made certain about its reputation for 'godliness and good learning'.

Of formal qualifications and letters after her name Miss Pierce had none, but she had other qualities that served her well: a

Ken (on the left) with his
elder brother, Ron, in 1925

commanding presence, the ability to sense what was going on behind her back, a rock-firm belief in herself and her values. She might perhaps have been induced to believe that there was a brand of education that claimed to be 'child centred'; that some infant schools stooped to sand trays and other toys; that in many schools copybooks and copper-plate writing had given way to Marion Richardson's neat script; and that drama, discussion and oral work generally now held a recognized place in the repertoire of modern educational methods. But if any breath of such heresies ever reached her, she showed little sign of it. To me, as to my parents, 'school' meant Miss Pierce's, and none of us had any idea that a school might ever be run in a different way from hers.

For two years I laboured in that well-lit schoolroom, learning to read, write, spell and 'do sums'. Reading and writing came with little effort, and spelling with little more, despite the potential confusion arising from dubious mnemonics that we were taught, such as 'I before E except after C'. There were few books in the school and I rarely did much reading in the classroom, but Miss Pierce asked us from time to time what we were reading at home. By the time I was seven I had fallen in love with the Sherlock Holmes stories. All too few of them came my way, but I read every one I could get hold of. So in response to her question, I confessed this passion one day to Miss Pierce. She drew herself up, beady eyes glistening through her gold pince-nez, and asked 'And what does that teach you?'

I felt a tremor of dismay. I had forgotten that her attitude towards literature was that if it was not 'improving' it was worthless. Not that she had ever said so explicitly, but it was clear enough. I fought to find a credible answer, but in a moment, all of Conan Doyle's plots had evaporated. 'Well,' I offered lamely, 'these stories teach you to look for clues.'

'And in what way?'

'Well, Miss, you can tell where people have been by the mud on their shoes.'

Most of the questions put to me in school, however, called for instant regurgitation rather than thought. From time to time religious instruction was conducted by Miss Pierce by a catechetical method. Every boy and girl in the room was called to form a great semicircle round her desk. The child on her right was 'top', the one on her left, 'bottom'. How we were first ranged in order, I can't recall, except that I see myself, as a new boy, on the left among the lowest of the low. The lesson went like this. The boy on my right was asked:

'What was Adam made of?'

'Dust, Miss.'

'Correct. Move up one.'

Then it was my turn to answer:

'What was Eve made of?'

'Adam's fifth rib, Miss.'

'Correct. Move up one.'

At the end of the lesson we numbered off, and our 'places' were recorded in the register – and in our memories. Spelling and mental arithmetic were conducted on similar lines, the latter a taxing exercise for non-computational wits such as mine, but a welcome relief from the endless exercises in Charles Pendlebury's *A Shilling Arithmetic*. In adult life, as a publisher of schoolbooks, I was always acutely aware of the importance of published prices, but this was one of the few I came across in which the price was announced in the title, apparently as the book's main recommendation.

Miss Daisy Pierce was a Presence of whom every child in her care went in awe. Occasionally she would rap a boy's hands with her ruler, but generally a single glance was enough to quell incipient trouble. We all agreed that she was 'strict', and we all waited for the day when we would go upstairs into the care of the other teacher in that school, Miss Jennison, who was said to be much more human.

A flight of stairs of scrubbed wood led to a landing on which there was a lavatory plentifully supplied with window-panes in its doors and walls, all covered with translucent patterned paper of a kind then common, but never seen today. This lavatory acquired unpleasant memories for me, for in it I once conducted a long imaginary conversation, attracting the attention first of pupils and then of Miss Pierce herself, all wondering how two people could be literally closeted together. Accustomed as I had become at home to enact my dramas in the security of the loo, I had not reckoned with the frailty of construction of the school's early-nineteenth-century convenience; and it was a long time before I lived down my unwelcome notoriety as the boy who made Miss Pierce run upstairs and rattle the door of the you-know-what.

Beyond the landing, however, were more stairs that led to the promised land, the classroom of Miss Jennison, which was in fact little more than a large attic. Looking back, I realize what an impossible task she was faced with, for she had two (and perhaps more) distinct groups of pupils to cope with simultaneously. First there were the seven- and eight-year-olds; then there were the 'big girls', the female pupils whose parents kept them on until they reached or passed the statutory leaving age of fourteen. We youngsters were supposed to get on with work that we were assigned, closing our ears to what was being said to and by the 'big girls'. But that, of course, was impossible, especially when they were doing such things as play-reading. There still rings in my head Miss Jennison's despairing threat that she would abandon the play altogether if one girl were to say even once more 'Percyphone' instead of 'Per-seph-o-ne'.

Yet, absurd though the conditions were, Miss Jennison was still on the right side of that mysterious boundary between youth and middle age, and still ready to try to cope with the near-impossible. I have a vision of her tripping down Guildhall Street to school on very high heels, her black cape flying in the wind, a tiny cap surmounting her sallow face – a faded and rather impoverished version of the 'flappers' or 'bright young things' of that period. 'Always the latest Paris fashions,' says Ron to me with a knowing man-of-the-world wink that makes me feel very much the younger brother; while in the background is a forest of timber scaffolding among which the lavatorially white-tiled frontage of the new Lefevre's store is rising to engulf the old Theatre Royal. Then I have another vision, of some forty years ago, during one of the annual festivals of the King's School. I see Miss Jennison painfully edging her way to a seat at an open-air performance of a Shakespeare play in one of the Cathedral canons' gardens. I watch her bask in the warmth of the sun and the pleasure of the performance. I feel an urge to go up to her and tell her I am one of her former pupils, and does she remember me? But without a word I let her shuffle away and out of my life for ever. Alas for British reserve, that consigns speech to water-closets and makes one tongue-tied in the open air!

Miss Jennison deserved my never-spoken gratitude. Once I had 'gone up' there was a wonderful change of climate. I felt I had left behind me the sterile grind and could now begin to use what I had learned. For the first time in my life, I was asked to write a story, recounting in my own words a fairy tale we had been told. To my amazement, my version was thought to be very good, and Miss Pierce came upstairs to hear it read aloud. It seemed I had differed from the others in introducing a lot of direct speech: perhaps my habit of conducting conversations in my head, which had had such embarrassing consequences in the school lavatory, had not been quite so pointless after all. But equally amazing was the quantity of red ink with which my essay was covered. Was it possible that I could ever master the complexities of quotation marks, question marks and all those other minute details that adults knew so well when and where to use? Triumph battled with despair – but should the young be insulated from such conflicts, denied a glimpse of the hard way ahead?

In other ways, too, my schooling seemed to be moving from winter into spring. Poetry made its first appearance. Nelson's 'History Readers', with pictures in full colour, introduced me to Alfred and the cakes and other absorbing folk tales, the mistletoe that sprouts from the limbs of history; and, above all, there was drawing and painting, in which I revelled even though we copied from illustrations rather than working from life.

How did these two ladies, unqualified save by their own sound but limited education and by their belief in themselves, educate between them some sixty or seventy children aged from five to fifteen? Given the conditions they worked in, how did they manage to cope with their near-impossible task? How did this disparate pair first come together, and how did they plan each day's campaign as they sat in the creamy glow reflected from Bell Harry's south face which pervaded Miss Pierce's parlour? Of these late-afternoon deliberations, carried out over Earl Grey tea and Madeira cake and punctuated every quarter an hour by the Cathedral clock, I shall never know anything. But I might have done, if only I had had the sense to speak to Miss Jennison in her old age. Such missed chances are ghosts that haunt one's latter years.

Whatever fascinating detail I might have gleaned from her, however, I feel sure that in the end everything she said would have converged to one point – the indomitable character and resolve of Miss Daisy Pierce. In some strange way her ruler, that wand of authority of fine boxwood marbled with many a stain of Stephens's red and blue-black inks, was symbolic of her person and her way of life: worn with use yet carefully preserved, upright, undeviating, almost two-dimensional, continually double-under-lining what was 'correct'.

In every aspect of her running of the school there was evidence of the steely core that underlay her formidable exterior; and this was seen nowhere more clearly than in the changing room at dis-missal time. At times she would enter, head held even higher than usual and ostentatiously sniffing. Maiden lady she might be, but she charged headlong into areas that some might have thought the exclusive preserve of mothers. 'Who's done something?' she would ask; and before long her moral authority would extort a reluctant confession of soiled pants. The matter did not rest there. 'Tell your mother …' began a familiar sermon, the peroration of which was on the necessity of washing the affected underclothes, and firm advice that simply drying things would not do – a com-plete change was necessary. That such child-borne advice might be resented by parents who paid in guineas for a genteel style of education, and that some of these might be tempted to 'take their child away' at the end of the term, worried her not a bit – or at any rate not visibly.

For any such disaffected parents there were plenty of alter-natives. There was a cluster of schools named after saints – St Christopher's, St Ninian's, St Bede's – which, moreover, had playgrounds. Another, Chaucer House in St George's Place, had no playground but it did boast teachers with Froebel certificates, who no doubt would have had nothing to do with pothooks and

The original Simon Langton Schools (boys' and girls' grammar schools) were adjacent and within the city walls. After they were destroyed by bombing in 1942 they were rebuilt on separate greenfield sites outside the city

hangers. Above all, there were the Langton and other local secondary schools, nearly all of which had 'junior' or 'preparatory' departments which seemed to offer an easily opened back door into the main school. This was the route my parents chose for me. Just before I was nine years old, I entered the Simon Langton Boys' School in May 1928, and there I was to stay for the next ten years.

What did I take with me as I passed from the domain of Miss Pierce and Miss Jennison to that much larger school? I had had four years of slaving to copy pothooks and hangers, of chanting multiplication tables, of puzzling over those mysteriously leaking water tanks in Pendlebury's *Arithmetic*, of constantly overhearing the 'big girls' getting their last hope of 'refinement' from Miss Jennison in the shape of fragmented French and smatterings of Shakespeare. Had it done me any good? Had it deadened my soul? Had I been the victim of unqualified amateurs who called themselves teachers but used methods that were even then antiquated and discredited?

No such doubts troubled me at any time in my young days or later. When I looked from the Dane John to see the children of St Mildred's Primary School at play on the hillock where their little Victorian Gothic school stood, it seemed as if I were gazing at the centre of a flower alive with insects, and for a moment or two I yearned to be one of that swarm. If only Miss Pierce's had had a playground! But my feelings of envy quickly evaporated. I knew I had been happy at Miss Pierce's, despite all the drudgery and the close confinement – but why?

Part of the answer is, I think, that each and every one of the fifty or sixty pupils in that little school had a sense of being watched, assessed and, when the right moment arrived, praised. There was, too, a strange and fruitful symbolism in the very structure of the school. When we 'went upstairs' from the classroom with its huge plate-glass windows, to enter the dark servants' garret over which Miss Jennison presided, it seemed something more than a merely physical elevation. The toil of our early years now had its reward. Exciting novelties came our way – not only painting in watercolour, but also making sculptures of Plasticene and some scented, malleable material called 'Glitter-wax'; while the enactments by the 'big girls' of classic myths and episodes from Shakespeare provided us with an alternative curriculum often more compelling than the tasks in which we were supposed to be totally absorbed.

On these two floors above Skinners' drapery shop there were two little worlds of effort and discovery almost cut off from the world of everyday life whose wheels and footsteps could be heard in moments of 'inattentiveness'. Yet not always and absolutely cut off, for there came a day, three years after I left, when history was made in Guildhall Street. Miss Pierce was far too good a teacher to let slip such an opportunity. Not a glimpse of the street could be seen through the plate-glass windows of the main classroom, so she gathered as many of her pupils as possible at the sash windows in the rest of the house, to watch out for an open car that would soon drive past on its way to Palace Street and the Deanery. In it sat a bespectacled Indian man clad in a voluminous white cotton *dhoti*. Our Member of Parliament, Sir William Wayland, had described him as 'a half demented fanatic', and the Cathedral clergy had spurned an invitation to meet him at the Deanery, where he would be staying as the guest of the new Dean, Hewlett Johnson. But Miss Pierce had no such scruples: history came only rarely to Guildhall Street, and she made sure that her pupils should have a chance to see Mahatma Gandhi as he passed by her door.

3

Wheels

WHAT WAS IT that drew me, very early in my life, to the Sherlock Holmes stories? I think it was partly because, in the earlier ones at least, the whole background to life was different to mine in one crucial respect – there were no motor cars, no rubber tyres travelling along the roads (with the important exception, of course, of bicycles). These tales belonged to a different stage of civilization to my own, a time when all long-distance travel by road relied on the iron-shod wheels of horse-drawn vehicles or railways.

Life had changed irrevocably since Holmes's and Watson's early adventures, yet however vividly I might be aware of the decline and fall of horse-going ways, living on St George's Terrace I found constant reminders that this had taken place only quite recently and was still not yet complete. Some of these reminders were at the front end of the house: the great granite horse trough, for instance, at the corner of Upper Bridge Street and St George's Street, where you could so often see carthorses refreshing themselves amid the petrol fumes. But the sense of old and new mingling was strongest at the back of the house, in St George's Lane, which ran parallel to the Terrace, and in my father's Mews of which the rear entrance was at the Lane's end.

Our back gate opened on a narrow, brick-lined passage which turned at a right angle to tunnel through a row of cottages and emerge in the Lane. Instantly, I was then in the domain of the horse. To the right, sandwiched between red-brick cottages of the nineteenth century and jettied houses of the sixteenth or seventeenth, were the great doors of the blacksmiths' forge. Perhaps Mr Burton and his colleague would have been better described as 'farriers' for they seemed to do nothing all day but shoe horses. Almost opposite were the quaintly timbered former stables of the Coach and Horses, an ancient coaching inn that stood on the corner of the Lane and the main street, to which it presented a time-worn face strangely contrasting with the red and gold of Woolworths' fascia next door. The coming of the railways in the 1840s and 1860s had destroyed the trade implicit in the inn's name, and the stables had fallen into decay; but until the bombs fell they were to have briefly a new lease of life as Peggy Court's school of dance. On the other corner of the lane-end was a cheap furniture shop whose hideous frontage and amazingly ugly stock accorded ill with the fact that this claimed to be the birthplace of Christopher Marlowe, who had been christened in St George's Church just across the narrow street.

The junction of St George's Lane and St George's Street was something to wonder at. On each side it was guarded by massive bollards of granite, and the Lane was so narrow – perhaps four feet – that I soon got into the habit of leaping from one kerbstone to the other as I passed down the main street. It was of course impossible for the Southern Railway's wagon to get through this eye of the needle, so whenever it approached this point – as it did continually in order to deliver crates of straw-packed earthenware and other heavy goods to the back entrance of Woolworths – the waggoner abandoned his high seat and backed until he reached the slightly wider roadway in front of the forge doors, where he had just room enough to turn round.

Emerging from the brick-tunnel into the Lane, I saw what was virtually its only element of modernity – Jennings's printing works. Through the open door I would often see the inheritor and prime mover of this establishment, who was later to become a notable Mayor of the city. Dark-haired, pencil-behind-ear, staccato of speech and movement, he briskly stacked newly printed copies of the *Kent Herald* on his counter to the tune of the incessant clatter of his presses. Their mechanical sound competed sometimes with doorstep chatter from aproned women in the cottages, or with greetings flung in an Irish accent to a jaunty little man whose slight bandiness and leather leggings announced him as an ostler. From behind the high wall adjoining Jennings's works there were also gusts of noise from 300 young Langton voices, starting and stopping as suddenly as if they had been under a conductor's baton. Thanks to Woolworths' insatiable need for stock, and the recurrent need of horses for shoes, there was the sound of hooves along the Lane throughout the year; but for a brief period each autumn this rose to a crescendo as the oast house at the other end of the Lane awoke to life. Load after load of enormous 'pockets' of hops, full to bursting, swung on its crane into the gloomy interior. Soon its fire was lit and the delicious scent of drying hops tinged the October air. A chain of these great incense-burners celebrated the festival of the hop harvest throughout the southern sector of the city, at Oaten Hill and St Lawrence Forstal, and further out at Stuppington, Wincheap and Cockering. My friends told me how, if you made friends with an 'oastie' – the guardian of the fire – he would pop your potatoes in the ashbox of the furnace and bake them to perfection undreamed-of; but how to strike up such a friendship with a man who worked twenty-four hours a day during his brief period of duty, taking only cat naps, was never explained.

Today the 'lanes' of old Canterbury survive as names of roads, but nearly always nowadays these roads take two 'lanes' of traffic. No such ambiguity was possible with the lanes of old – feeble growths that branched off the stem of the main street. Any thought of passing a stationary vehicle in St George's Lane, Canterbury Lane, Burgate Lane, Rose Lane or Iron Bar Lane was out of the question. These lanes were alleyways rather than roads: Iron Bar Lane, in fact, burrowed its way under the first floor of buildings in the main street; it was suitable for pedestrians, pack horses and just the occasional wheeled vehicle which ventured into its close embrace.

Horse-drawn traffic was dying but not dead. The incessantly busy blacksmiths' shop was evidence of that. It drew me like a magnet from my earliest acquaintance with the Lane. I was not alone: there was nearly always a group of wide-eyed children clustered round the doors, sometimes so numerous that they had to be warned by the smiths not to advance too far, and sometimes even told to go away. I never saw any of the finer parts of the blacksmith's art practised here: there was no shaping of graceful scrolls or fashioning of filigree of leaves and tendrils. These two elderly men in leather aprons, one massive and stern, the other slighter, grey-haired and benign, seemed to have only one task – the making and fitting of horseshoes. Length after length of iron bar was heated, a piece cut off, unmeasured but always accurate, and while still glowing was shaped into a crescent on the beak of the anvil. A few pulls on the handle of the bellows, and the forge fire blazed and then subsided into a red glow; in went the half-made shoe, to emerge for further shaping and for the nail holes to be punched through it. Then came the climax: one of the smiths, nearly always the older man, advanced, nails in his mouth, to lift one of the great carthorse's now unshod hooves into his lap. Hot but not glowing, the newly made shoe made contact with the nerveless face of the hoof: an acrid burning smell, by no means unpleasant, arose amid blue smoke, and once the smith was satisfied, the nails were hammered home. Sometimes a horse was restive: what if it were to lash out and take the smith unawares? But he always seemed to be in command, stilling any sign of rebellion with a muttered growl, until he calmly finished the operation with a few strokes of the rasp and a burnishing of the hoof.

Absorbing though I found this spectacle, it was in my own father's life and work that I saw most clearly how horse-going ways, even if in decline, were still far from extinction. Above all, this was visible in the Mews – an acre or thereabouts of yards, stables and garages stretching from the main entrance on Watling Street to the double doors at the rear which faced down St George's Lane. Adjoining this rear entrance there was a collection of tarred timber buildings in Gravel Walk that seemed to have come straight out of some farmyard. Such pockets of rurality did not seem strange in a city that still contained many secluded gardens and hidden open spaces, a few of which remain even today despite the ubiquitous threat of tarmac. Once through the gate, the farmyard impression was intensified by the stench of the great manure-heap – the 'maxel', I think my father called it, though I have not found the word in any dictionary. Here indeed was the domain of the horse, and one of the last lairs of the leather-gaitered legion who were master and servant to that noble animal.

As we entered, one of this tribe would waddle from his harness-hung cubicle in the corner, a place of high-Victorian discomfort whose flagstones and hard chair were tempered only by the cherry-red glow of a coal fire and some source of inner warmth which battled against the maxel-fumes as he spoke. From the stable doorways adjoining his little room I could hear the occasional kick of a hoof against the massive partitions, the rustle of straw, and sometimes a whinny. Soon we would go in, me keeping well clear of rear hooves and my father administering the odd apple or sugar lump, alert for any problem that might call for the administration of white oils. This was a salve obtainable from Mr Field, the saddler in Dover Street, which even in its milder form prepared for human use could set one's muscles on fire, fighting pain with pain. Otherwise he might prescribe a diet of bran mash, or a rest from work, or a visit from the vet. There were perhaps a dozen horses there, not drays, but each powerful enough to pull the flat wagons by which coal and other fuels were delivered all over the city throughout the 1920s and 1930s and on into the post-war years.

These deliveries of fuel were the main job for this team of horses, but at a glance one could see what other tasks might come their way, from household removals of the humbler sort to waiting at stations between the shafts of a cab, from funerals to festive excursions into the city's hinterland. Beyond the stables were huge garages, some with sliding doors and others open-fronted, and yet others rented out as lock-up garages to commercial firms such as Lyons and Brooke Bond. Tucked in one corner was the waggonette, a large canvas-roofed cart with two facing rows of wooden seats along its length. It was now a curiosity, almost an antique, though I could well remember riding in it with a dozen others to some church anniversary at Broad Oak – a five-mile excursion there and back, with the fun of getting out and walking to help the horse get up Babs Oak Hill.

Hanging from the rafters of the Mews were a couple of 'tilts', covers of green canvas on wooden frames that could be fitted on to small lorries or carts, for small haulage jobs such as removals. And under shelter in the main part of the Mews or in one of its bays were the horse-drawn carriages, mostly closed landaus but including one or two with hoods that could be folded back in fine weather, which plied for hire from the railway stations or elsewhere by special order. One of these 'cabs' would take you quite a way within the city for a shilling, which was considerably less than the minimum charge of half-a-crown for a ride in a petrol-driven taxi, and on the special occasions when my father made a family excursion to the woods (there to combine business with pleasure by negotiating with a woodcutter for cordwood, poles, faggots or pea and bean sticks) there was infinite pleasure to be had from sitting high up alongside the driver, trundling along at little more than walking pace, so that every detail of the scene could be absorbed, and turning from time to time to address or question the others nestling in the well of the vehicle.

Already this mode of transport was in one sense defunct. I was dimly aware that new horse-drawn carriages were simply not being made. Not that there was any need to worry about that, for the supply of old ones seemed quite adequate to the demand; and if repairs of a major kind were needed, there was that fascinating place, the wheelwright's shop of Dent & Eaton in Puckle Lane, where from the doors you could see such marvels performed as the sweating of a new iron tyre on to a newly repaired wooden wheel. Even the renovation of bodywork was no great problem:

the coachbuilding establishment of W. S. Williams & Sons, 'established 1815', still functioned at the bottom end of Gravel Walk, a stone's throw from the Mews, carrying on the old tradition of applying coat after coat of paint, each rubbed down meticulously to achieve a depth and richness of colour that no cellulose spray has ever been able to surpass. Little did I think that the day would come when I would pay the latest and last of the coachbuilding Williamses to use this same technique to ensure that our first child should be transported in suitable luxury.

The patterns of life, of thought, of craftsmanship engendered by the horse-going era sank deep into the collective consciousness and, for a time at least, deeply influenced other modes of transport. When you travelled by train, right up to the middle of the twentieth century, the window was raised and lowered by a leather strap, and fastened shut by a hinged flap at its bottom – the whole mechanism being precisely that of a horse-drawn cab. Until recently, except in the latest rolling stock, the seating arrangements on the railways, with their cubicles in which passengers faced each other, echoed the layout of the horse-drawn carriages which, in the infancy of railways, were loaded entire on to railway wagons for the transport of their wealthier customers.

The same principle of 'copying the coachbuilders' could be seen in operation here in the Mews. For, turning away from the champing, scuffling and neighing of the stables, you saw a splendid collection of old cars, great unwieldy vehicles, mostly of pre-1914 vintage, none of which I ever saw burst into life, for they were of makes that had passed into limbo, and spares were unobtainable. Why they stayed there was a mystery locked in the breast of my father's admirable associate, Arthur Kelway, who was effectively foreman of the Mews and who looked after all things mechanical. They disappeared at last, I think, only in the 1950s, before their value as vintage cars could be seen. Each one of these vehicles was clearly a 'horseless carriage'. They were all much taller than modern cars, so that passengers stepped into them only slightly flexed, not folded almost double. Each was spacious, with an interior like a padded room; and of course details such as window-straps were precisely as in horse-drawn carriages. The driver's seat was not quite as exposed as that of the unfortunate 'cabbie', but it was half-open to the elements and separated from the passengers by a soundproof but openable glass screen. Above all, there was virtually no attempt at streamlining. True, one of these ancient cars, I think a Renault, had a radiator that did not have a vertical front but rose without any grille in a graceful ogee towards the windscreen; but I felt then (as I do still) that aesthetics rather than engineering dictated its form.

Who was I, at the age of nine or ten, to be passing judgment on the aesthetics of car design? The fact was that if ever I were to be interested in ideas about form and function, cars would inevitably be my starting-point, for nothing else in my universe was of more absorbing interest. There were many reasons for this. Mass production methods were beginning to pour cars on to the roads: they were no longer the toys of the rich and the well-to-do, but were beginning to be attainable objects of desire for ordinary people. Just how this flood was mounting, we schoolboys could easily see as we 'collected' registration numbers, eagerly watching as the numbers prefixed by the letters 'FN', which Canterbury had used ever since cars were born, mounted towards the fateful total of 9999, when a new start would have to be made. This happened around 1930, and a new prefix, 'JG', then replaced 'FN'; and during the 1930s we progressively lost interest in number plates as AFN, AJG, BFN, and almost every other conceivable permutation was used up with ever-increasing speed.

What I and my friends had grasped, with naïve intuition, was that suddenly the car had found an identity of its own; that its designers and manufacturers had broken free of allegiance to the idea of the horseless carriage and were producing art-forms of a kind that the world had not seen before. Furthermore, there was a great range of makers, each one truly individual. The merging of smaller firms into a few vast, monolithic blocks had then hardly begun. There were names that spoke of quality such as Lanchester;

there was the irresistibly 'sporty' image that the initials 'MG' conjured up (we did not realize that this was part of Sir William Morris's empire); there was the range of Austin cars, from the stately saloons to the immensely popular little 'Seven' (the butt of innumerable music-hall jokes), all claiming to be 'the dependable car'; there was that rather strange firm, Singer, always experimenting with new body shapes and claiming to be producing 'the car of the future'; there were exciting imports in plenty from America, such as the numerous Essex Super Sixes with their distinctive white-walled tyres; and there were those magnificent Rileys with their fabric-covered bodies which sloped steeply at the rear, giving them an air of speed and sprightliness that was justified by their performance – a retired bishop recently described how, as a schoolboy in 1933, he egged the chauffeur of the family's Riley to touch the top speed of 72 m.p.h. between Canterbury and Bridge, on the understanding that nothing should be said to his father.

Variety, individuality, change, unpredictability – such were the characteristics of those heady years of car manufacture midway between the wars. My friends and I eagerly studied every car catalogue we could get hold of, and glued our noses to the showrooms of Barretts, near the Westgate, and the Invicta Motor Company in Lower Bridge Street. It was from the Invicta that I first learned epoch-making news – the Model T Ford was to be discontinued and replaced by something utterly different and as yet secret: the Model E. Now, the Model T was part of our lives – tall, black, spiky, it had poured out in its thousands from Detroit ever since Henry Ford established the first mass-production line in the world in 1913. It was the original 'Tin Lizzie', to be seen in every Laurel and Hardy film (once, in an unforgettable sequence, being sawn in half by the bandsaw of a timber factory). It was a basic car, reliable yet crude. Henry Ford's observation that it was available in any colour so long as it was black did not seem to us in any way funny or objectionable; but to our sophisticated young eyes, the Model T had one great stylistic fault: that the roof and the rear wall of the body met in a sharp edge like the lid of a biscuit tin, or the top of a landau, instead of the smooth curve that, in our eyes, modernity demanded.

But all this was about to be changed. Weeks ahead of the great day, there were warning announcements in the Invicta windows; days ahead there was the actual car, heavily veiled so that not an inch of it should be seen prematurely; and then at last on a spring day in 1928 the Model E was revealed, not black but in glorious Technicolor, with 'wire wheels' of many thin spokes instead of a few thick bar-spokes, and with a body shape that was much more curvaceous and alluring than Auntie Lizzie's strait-backed image. If anyone had tried to convey to me what the word 'revolution' meant, their best chance of success would have been by comparing Model E with Model T.

Very rapidly I became adept at identifying the model and year of almost any car I saw, even when I had only the glimpse of a mudguard or headlamp to go by; and to this day I find myself thinking as a vintage car goes by, 'Austin Twelve, 1926', or some such formula. But there is never anyone at hand capable of checking the accuracy of my reflexes as my friends constantly did.

This grand passion developed almost into a religion, and soon I was provided with a temple. In 1930 our family moved to a new house in New Dover Road. I had long been aware that this road began with a tall and very long brick wall that stretched right round the corner into Upper Chantry Lane. Someone told me that this was Ersham Lodge, until recently the home of the Earl of Guilford. Soon a breach appeared in the walls, through which I could see the early Victorian mansion, already derelict among a rampant growth of what had once been a fine and spacious garden, an urban oasis in which the Earl had lived in stately seclusion, set apart from commoners living close by in the fourteenth-century cottages of Chantry Lane (all to be destroyed in the war, including the one claimed to be the ''umble 'ome' of Uriah Heep).

On part of that garden, fronting on to New Dover Road but set well back from it, arose not merely a building but a new kind of building – a purpose-built, architect-designed car showroom commissioned by the firm of Maltbys, who still clung to their ancient description as 'coachbuilders'. Maltbys had established themselves in Canterbury in the early 1920s, in a tiny seventeenth-century shop on the corner of All Saints Lane, just beyond the narrowest part of the main street at Kings Bridge. It would be hard to imagine any premises less suitable for a car showroom. But Maltbys evidently learned from this mistake. After nearly a decade in their cramped premises, they commissioned an architect named Eric Randerson (a local lad who had made good, my grandfather approvingly observed) to design a new showroom and service centre on the corner of the Ersham Lodge garden at the junction of New Dover Road and Upper Chantry Lane.

Randerson faced a difficult question: what form should a car showroom take? There was no widely accepted answer to this, any more than there is to the question today of what a supermarket should look like. The young architect found his inspiration in ancient Greece. Massive pillars of fine sandstone rose to frame enormous plate-glass windows; all the detailing was of true classical provenance, even down to the urns that crowned the corners

Maltbys purpose-built car showroom appeared on the corner of New Dover Road and Upper Chantry Lane in 1931. The site remained a garage until the 1980s

of the roofline, and there was a row of petrol pumps with the workshop and stores department behind them. To boyish eyes at least, the showroom seemed to be at least a quarter of an acre in extent, with light flooding in from the great windows and, halfway up the back wall, a balcony to enable the array of cars to be seen from above.

Was it grand, or was it ridiculous? Opinions might differ, but so potent was the image of this building that when, many years later, it was bought by a furniture company, the planners insisted that the grand classically porticoed frontage should be retained. Unfortunately, by one of those accidents that so often seem to frustrate the best efforts of conservationists, this splendid façade was accidentally destroyed by the new owners. No matter: a more-or-less accurate replica was improvised. But reader beware: what you can see today is no true relic of Maltbys' glory – it is not sandstone, but *fibreglass*, though a reminder still of the temple that once stood here.

Appropriately enough, at the centre of this temple I found a goddess – a huge Minerva saloon car. This was succeeded after a time by an equally big Delage, but after these long-forgotten deities came a host of lesser but longer-lasting names – above all, Morris – catering neither for Earls nor for Uriah Heeps, but for a large section of humanity between these two extremes. The high-water mark of this tide of democracy was reached about 1936, when with a great flourish Morris brought the dream of the 'hundred pound car' into the realm of reality. This little black two-seater seemed to me a poor thing, in which looks and comfort had been mercilessly sacrificed on the altar of cheapness. Not for this, surely, had Maltbys' temple been built. But the great British public liked the idea that a new car could be had for so little money – maybe £6,000 or £7,000 in today's money – and soon there was a family saloon on the market at the same price, the Ford Popular, which offered even better value.

These little cars, despised by us but not by the car-envying general public, helped to drive home the message that cars were no longer just the plaything of the rich. Traffic increased, so that at peak times there always had to be white-gloved policemen on 'point duty' doing their elaborate, swift drill of directing traffic at St George's and St Margaret's Streets and other traffic nodes. Around 1930, however, a strange new device was installed at the former of these two junctions. It was called 'traffic lights', and its meaning had to be mastered. It was easy enough to see what the red and green lights meant: even so, they were marked at first with the words 'Stop' and 'Go', but the light between these two was a bit puzzling – even its name, which we thought should be 'orange', was 'amber'. About the same time, the taxi-rank that had existed in St George's Place as far back as I could remember was abolished. I was sad about that because it meant that I no longer saw a taxi-man of very distinctive appearance. This man sported upswept moustaches, and his clothes vaguely suggested a military uniform. His position was very close to the fine Georgian house of Dr Lucas, who was known as 'the flying doctor' because he sometimes used his private aeroplane to visit distant patients – eventually having a fatal accident. Rumour had it that the moustachioed driver had been Dr Lucas's batman during the Great War.

The introduction of traffic lights and the removal of long-established taxi-ranks were among a host of novelties due to the growing flood of traffic. One such newcomer was the flashing orange globes at each side of a pedestrian crossing. For many years these were known as 'Belisha Beacons' on account of the fact that they were introduced while Leslie Hore-Belisha was transport minister. Yet despite all these changes, traffic was seen by many, and especially by tradespeople, as an opportunity rather than a problem. Road transport brought hordes of shoppers into the city from the surrounding villages, particularly towards the end of the week. A large yellow sign on the railway bridge at Wincheap blazoned the message 'William Lefevre Ltd for the best part of your shopping', and a similar message inscribed on the wall of my grandparents' house at Blean not only brought in a rewarding fee – but also saved them considerable redecorating costs.

In 1930 the secretary of the Chamber of Trade at Canterbury

remarked that 'the omnibus services are certainly strangling trade in the villages'. This was merely the first stage, however, in a process that has gone on ever since, enormously accelerated by the coming of supermarkets, which has changed villages from being almost self-sufficient communities into mere residential satellites of towns.

Bringing shoppers in by bus incurred few environmental problems apart from the fact that these large vehicles might sometimes score the sides of the Westgate Towers – car traffic, though, was a different matter. As far back as 1905 the antiquary J. C. Cox had written 'whatever may be said in favour of the new method of locomotion, so popular with certain of the wealthy few, the presence of these throbbing, noisy, evil-smelling machines is eminently offensive to all, save the selfish occupants, in the narrow streets of old-world Canterbury', and he went on to suggest that motorists should be induced to leave their cars outside the city.

About eighty years after this tirade, the city began to act on it by relying increasingly on the principle of 'park and ride' to get shoppers and visitors into the centre without their cars. In the meantime, the main stress was on accommodating and regulating car traffic rather than excluding it. A dreadful accident on King's Bridge in 1930, when a car somehow pulled a woman to the ground and ran over her head, did not lead to a call for a ban on city-centre traffic, but caused some to urge afresh the need for a 'relief road' to siphon off the 'through' traffic heading for Thanet. In 1931 the *Kentish Gazette* twice published a sketch map showing how this road would bypass the village of Sturry and eliminate waits at the railway level crossing. Even today there is a gap in Whitstable Road where the new road should have come through – but nothing ever happened, and Sturry still waits for its bypass. Others argued that, to relieve congestion, cars should be allowed to park on only one side of the main street. But which side? No agreement could be reached on that question, since traders feared that having parked on one side the occupants of the car would do all their shopping on that same side and not cross the road!

Amid all this beating about the bush, only two positive moves to cope with the problem of traffic in the city centre can be discerned. The first was the banning of street traders' barrows, together with instructions to the 'constables' to tell motorists to 'come in' – that is, to park close to the kerb. The Town Clerk in 1930 was Henry Fielding, a descendant of the novelist of the same name, and his newly appointed successor seems to have been conscious of his literary heritage, so one of his first bye-laws began with suitable sonority:

> Whereas the streets set out in the schedule hereto are between the hours of eleven in the forenoon and eight in the afternoon thronged and liable to be obstructed every day of the week ...

They don't make bye-laws quite like that nowadays!

The other effort to cope with traffic problems was the widening of Broad Street to make it live up to its name, and, as part of the same scheme, the creation of the city's first purpose-built car park. Mid-summer of 1931 saw a remarkable commemoration of this achievement, a ceremony that was witnessed by most of the mayors of Kentish towns and a horde of spectators so numerous that some were perched on rooftops. This multitude was addressed by the Minister of Public Works, George Asbury, who had come 'at great personal inconvenience' (said the press reports) straight from a Cabinet meeting. To the surprise of many, he had little to say about roads and traffic, but chose instead to praise the city's fine record in providing affordable housing for low-income families. It is safe to say, however, that not one of his hearers was in any doubt that car-borne traffic, commodious car parks and new urban roads were all Good Things. Two years previously, the chairman of the Chamber of Trade, Mr Wright Hunt, presiding over a debate about the perennial question of the coming Channel Tunnel, concluded that 'there could be no doubt that Canterbury would benefit very considerably by the increased traffic'. Exactly fifty years later, the then chairman of the Chamber said the same thing in almost the same words, but perhaps with not quite the same absolute degree of certainty.

We had no family car and my father seemed to show no inclination to learn to drive, though long after his death I learned that he had tried and then given up. This was a sadness that I shared with my friends. And yet it began to dawn on me that, however absolutely my father seemed to belong to the age of the horse, a large part of the growing prosperity that had lifted us out of our antiquated house into a new one in the suburbs could be summed up in one word: petrol.

This paradox was clearly symbolized at the entrance to the Mews in Watling Street. Let into the left-hand gatepost was a stone slab inscribed with the words 'Slater's Depository', followed by a late-nineteenth-century date in Roman numerals. The precise date I can't remember, but it belonged to the period when the supremacy of the horse was unchallenged. In human institutions, a sense of immortality seems generally to be the harbinger of decay and dissolution – and so it was with Slater's Depository, for it lasted only a few decades before my father bought the whole imposing premises, in the year of my birth, for what I can only suppose to have been a knock-down figure.

Everything about the Mews spoke of a mistaken belief in the permanence of horse-going ways – its extent, its lavish construction, the fine detailing of the French-polished woodwork in the office, the craftsmanship of the mahogany and plate-glass rostrum which now stood, dusty and abandoned, in a corner. For this place had been set up as a centre for horse auctions, generating a substantial turnover for a time and enabling the owner to build a handsome Victorian house next to it, facing towards Dane John, in which his daughter, heiress to a diminished asset, now lived a solitary existence.

A few yards behind the tablet announcing so confidently the establishment of the Depository there stood the symbol of its decline and fall, an 'Aunt Sally' (as I had learned to call it from the

'W. E. Pinnock's Taxi Fleet' says the caption on this postcard from the 1920s. Arthur Kelway stands on the running board, yet his cap is still below the roofline. Such tall taxis remained in use in Canterbury until the 1960s

pages of Arthur Mee's weekly *Children's Newspaper*) – a body-shaped mechanism painted green, with a long 'neck' of steel tubing surmounted by a globe of white frosted glass. From this ugly, hand-cranked pump flowed the life-blood of my father's growing business. The one scrap that I possess of his accounts shows that in the early 1920s he was using hundreds of gallons a year. No doubt the taxis shown in the recently reissued postcard of 'W. E. Pinnock's fleet' – those same taxis that later rested immobile for so many years under the Mews roof – accounted for a good part of the total. But undoubtedly most went into the tanks of the lorries.

There was first of all the two-tonner, a giant for those days but tiny by today's standards, its radiator adorned with vertical ribs on which were imposed 'Tilling Stevens' and 'Petrol-Electric'. They were magic words for which I never sought a meaning, for the instant the starting-handle was swung they performed an incantatory dance to the throbbing music within. Just as robust, but slighter, were the 30 cwt (and here I must interpose the explanation that 'cwt' was pronounced 'hundredweight') Ford lorries that delivered fuel along narrow country roads. But near the end of the 1920s these were replaced by a new breed, the sleek, sophisticated Chevrolets, with engines that purred rather than rattled and with radiators that looked just like larger versions of American saloon cars – or 'sedans' as they were called, retrieving a word that had dropped out of current English. As I rode in comfort alongside one of the drivers, 'Chev' Newington, as he was called in honour of his vehicle, I congratulated myself on the firm's emergence from the barbarism of the solid-tyred era; and within the Mews itself I saw constant evidence of the power of petrol, in the form of the majestic vans of J. Lyons & Co., resplendent in gold and blue, or the nippy little red Trojan vans powered by two-stroke engines operating a chain drive like the lawnmowers of that day. Here were two competing firms, each with its own artistic style – Lyons with its sumptuously baroque livery, and Brooke Bond stylishly modern with its Plantin upper and lower case lettering, white thinly outlined in black against a vivid red background – and each finding a totally different answer to the question of what was the most economic kind of vehicle to pour this wonder-working stuff, petrol, into. Here in Watling Street, which once had resounded to the tramp of the legions and in centuries since to the clatter of hooves, I was seeing a revolution now well into its stride, presenting its participants with all sorts of new questions in the fields of engineering, logistics and even aesthetics.

Questions – that was one of the features of this new post-horse age. One day at the Mews I found my father and Mr Kelway in deep discussion. Arthur Kelway was a man of parts – not only taximaster and engineer, but signwriter as well. Some strange instinct had given me, even by the age of ten, a keen interest in letterforms, and with the professionalism of Lyons and Brooke Bond in the back of my mind I sometimes watched with a sinking heart as Mr Kelway patiently drew the name 'W. E. PINNOCK Ltd.' on a lorry door to encircle the legend 'Tel. 358'. My dismay was due to the fact that he had a way of introducing a point, like the beginning

WANTED, Experienced Driver for Heavy Lorry, and a Lorry Driver's Mate. Also a good Horse Driver and a strong, willing Youth who wants to make headway. Permanent jobs for suitable applicants. An Odd Man, useful for whole or part-time work, is also required. — Apply W. E. Pinnock Ltd., 32, Dover Street, Canterbury.

This advert, from a 1920s street directory, shows that Ken's father had negotiated a deal with the railway company. Horse-drawn carriages were still commonplace at that time

of a bud, midway along what should have been the uninterrupted circumference of the letter 'O', and of scalloping all vertical and diagonal strokes of letters. In short, I detected signs of the sin of Victorianism.

But there came a day when Mr Kelway's signwriting concerned something far more substantial than mere artistic style. As he and my father bent their heads over an enormous layout, I saw that it was for the firm's new fascia board, to be executed in shadowed lettering and fixed at the front edge of the slated roof of the Mews, to be read at fifty yards' distance from the entrance in Watling Street. At such a distance, telegraphese was necessary. 'Coal, Coke and Wood Merchants' was first decided on, followed by 'Road Haulage, Household Removals, Taxi cabs, Charabancs'. But that last word posed awful problems. To begin with, there was only one of them, a red beast with a brass radiator labelled boldly 'Bean', with non-communicating rows of seats sloping upwards from front to rear as in a theatre, each row being accessed by its own door on right or left. Artistic licence would surely justify the use of the plural, even to my father's sensitive conscience. The trouble was, the spelling. 'Chars-a-bancs' seemed too French; 'Charabancs' might be incorrect. I wish I could remember which was actually chosen. There was a similar problem over the pronunciation of the word 'garage'. Was it 'garage', à la Française, or was it 'garridge'? Gradually the latter prevailed.

These were trifles, but they were symptomatic of the way in which continually and insistently the internal combustion engine posed totally new questions that the wise – particularly the commercially wise – would try to answer. One such question was naturally the extent to which the new form of transport should displace the old. Despite his reliance on petrol, my father's answer was that the horse-drawn flat trucks were still the best for local deliveries of coal, and even sometimes for small jobs such as minor household removals; and so on my visits to the Mews I could find delightful reminders of that age of the horse which, though visibly coming to an end, was still alive.

Muscle power, whether of horse or man, still counted. In the 'trade' section of local directories of the 1930s you can find listed a number of 'carriers' – a now long-extinct breed – some of whom had regular routes along which they went on prescribed days to deliver all sorts of heavy goods: items of furniture, spare parts for machines, parcels of household goods that the purchaser couldn't take by bus and train. There was, for instance, Fagg who operated from the Star Yard in Dover Street, close to the main entrance to the cattle market, covering Stelling Minnis and Upper and Lower Hardres. During the decade the name was changed from 'Star Yard' to 'Star Garage' and this no doubt signified the change from a wagon covered by a canvas tilt to a small lorry. Here, too, were a few travelling 'shops' which served the villages around Canterbury. By far the best known of these was the elaborately equipped horse-drawn vehicle which operated from its base at Goodman's hardware shop in Wincheap. It was stocked with every kind of household article – china of utilitarian sorts, baking tins, brooms, brushes, mops, scrubbing boards, dyes, nails at so much per pound, and a hundred other things. The scent of linoleum and its cheaper substitute, Congoleum, mingled with Sunlight Soap and paraffin (bring your own can, or buy one on the spot), and fought with the heady whiffs from the stable at the rear of Goodman's shop from which, every weekday, emerged the ebullient character universally known as 'Happy' – that is, Happy Hart – grasping his horse's halter. From the sides of the van hung tin kettles and every other sort of non-breakable and reasonably portable goods that the Wincheap shop had to offer; and almost buried within its array of shelves and cavities was a capacious paraffin tank that kept many a cottage lamp burning and fuelled the smelly two-burner stoves on which the farm-worker's dinner would be heated or re-heated to greet his return at the end of the day. Rain or fine, even when one winter a fellow-travelling helper suffered severe frostbite, Goodman's van ranged over a ten-mile radius from Wincheap. Defying the challenge of petrol, it continued into the post-war era when plastics, non-stick pans and bottled gas began to replace tin-plate, iron and paraffin.

Happy Hart may be taken as the outstanding example of the way in which mechanical power eventually, but by no means suddenly, won the victory over muscle power. Until the outbreak of war, and even to some extent after its end, the battle went on. Cabs as well as taxis attended the stations; and there was also a group of 'licensed porters' who operated from the stations, pushing heavy, two-wheeled flat trucks for sixpence or a shilling to any address in the city, fetching and carrying a traveller's trunks or other heavy goods. There was a multitude of tradesmen's bicycles, mostly ridden by whistling errand boys in their early teens, each equipped with a massive wicker basket at the front and with the name-plate of the business lettered on a metal plate within the frame of the cycle. Dry cleaners and other 'light' trades might use a motor-cycle, or cycle 'combinations' consisting of a bicycle attached to a side-car with a third wheel.

Most striking of all the changes brought by petrol were of course those in public transport. Only for a little while were we able to enjoy the delights of our little passenger trains along the Elham Valley line to Folkestone and the ancient 'Crab and Winkle' line, engineered by George Stephenson himself, to Whitstable. The lofty inhabitants of South Canterbury had to give up their five-minute journeys (only sevenpence, First Class) from the corrugated iron station of Canterbury South to Canterbury East or West, and take to the East Kent company's little red 'city' buses which seemed to scurry everywhere to and from the public houses named above their windscreens, such as 'Hop Poles' or 'Bat and Ball'. But why should I worry about that? On the other hand, it was a matter for real regret when the Whitstable rail service, which we knew as the 'Whitstable Bung', had to admit defeat. Its carriages, of pre-1914 vintage, still bore on every window a warning in English and French not to lean out of the windows (*Ne pas se pencher en dehors*), and I had absorbed, though not yet practised, the advice of my Whitstable school friends that it was possible to go into the tunnel and emerge as a black man – simply by leaving the window open. The journey itself was pure poetry – the dramatic plunge into darkness and then, after a short cutting which led to the tiny Blean Halt (it could never be dignified by the word 'station'), an embowered progress through the remoteness of Blean forest, suddenly rewarded by the sight and smell of the sea. No wonder that track has now been converted into a scenic path for walkers and cyclists.

Going by bus to Whitstable was a poor thing by comparison with the rail journey, but it was cheaper and the service was very frequent. There was an element of uncertainty and excitement about it, too, for around 1930 a 'pirate' line of buses started up in competition to the East Kent. The newcomers were in green livery and they belonged to a firm called 'Cambrian'. How such a remotely based bus company could have set up in our part of the world we youngsters did not bother about, but what we soon came to realize was that most of the conductors seemed to be very haphazard about collecting fares, especially from unaccompanied children. We surmised, probably correctly, that this laxity was designed to attract custom and so preserve jobs. The conductors had instinctively grasped one of the main principles of modern retailing, that by giving things away you can often secure the lasting loyalty of customers. Judging by the mechanical state of many of the buses, the company and its shareholders benefited little, and before long the East Kent's monopoly was ratified by new licensing legislation designed to regulate and control the growth of commercial traffic on the roads. But for us young travellers, travelling by pirate bus, usually at breakneck speed and often for nothing, was fun while it lasted.

In all sorts of ways, traffic, which today everyone agrees to be a pest except so far as one's own vehicle is concerned, was then a delight. I will single out just one element of that pleasure – the steam-driven lorries. Who, except the few who take an interest in 'period' transport, know anything about them? Yet they come irresistibly to mind, quietly hissing and chugging, with little emission of steam and only a small glow from their under-belly ashpits to indicate the source of power, as they wait to discharge a burden of Kent's Best to the Old City of Canterbury and many another city pub, or sack upon sack of Hovis flour to the warm bowels of Mr Peters's bakery on the corner of Old Dover Road and Oaten Hill. All of them, it seemed, were made by either Foden (a magic name to brass-band enthusiasts such as my family) or Sentinel. Only a select company of large firms ran them – brewers, millers and some large haulage contractors such as Bretts in Wincheap – probably because their servicing required specialized skills. Almost feminine in some ways, for they gave warning by a falsetto whistle instead of the baritone honk of a bulb-horn, they were in stark contrast to the older generation of steam-powered vehicles, the traction engines and rollers that clanked to and from Holmans' engineering works in Dover Street. 'Power without grace, force without flexibility' was the message about steam propulsion that their brutal progress seemed to spell out – and perhaps in the end the clean and sweetly running Fodens and Sentinels were condemned by association with these antiquated monsters rather than by any objective evidence. Whatever the reasons, they quietly vanished from the scene, along with the endless variety of muscle- and motor-powered side-car 'combinations' for commercial as well as private use, the legion of solid-tyred tricycles with insulated containers packed full of Wall's or Eldorado ice cream, and many another kind of traffic that travels now only along the roads of old people's memories.

For me, the fascination of the roads was confirmed, even canonized, by the family holiday we spent at Oxford in the summer of 1930. In those days, Oxford University slept the summer away, quads quiet, dons dozing, blinds drawn and curtains closed. Or so it seemed to my eleven-year-old eyes, as I gazed at the lawns of Christ Church where Alice Liddell had played while Dr Dodgson, lecturer in mathematics, wove the tale of her adventures in Wonderland. With my father's stories of Oxford in the 1880s ringing in my mind, it was easy enough to slip back in imagination to the Victorian age; and so it came as no great surprise one day to encounter my form master, Mr Whinfield, accompanied by two ladies – his sisters, I gathered later – who were dressed in the fashion of fifty years before: their high-pointed hats equipped with dark veils, their necks adorned with jet beads, and their skirts brushing the Cowley Road pavements. The Oxford of *Charley's Aunt* was evidently the Oxford of only yesterday.

Yet soon I got to know something of a very different Oxford – not the seat of learning, but the crucible of a new technology. I had often heard from my father how an obscure bicycle repairer named William Morris had built up the great car-making firm at Cowley, on the outskirts of the city. Now he took us to see it. How fascinating it was – the endless rows of cars on the production lines, the smell of upholstery and cellulose paint, the skill of the worker who painted hairlines of white on the newly finished car bodies with amazing accuracy and speed, the burly tyre fitter who disdained the use of tools to do a job that he could literally do by hand, the stories we heard of how Sir William himself would even now come into the factory, whip off his jacket and impetuously complete some job that others had been struggling with. We came away with catalogues of all the new models – the Cowley, Oxford, Isis, the open tourer (was British weather then what it has been ever since?), and I became an instant authority on all aspects of Morris cars. What a bore I must have been! But my ego was deflated as only boys of eleven know how. I can remember to this day the spot – a hundred yards east of Maltbys – that had sparked me off. Suddenly the two school friends who were with me chanted in unison 'When I was in Oxford', echoing the phrase I had been using to the point of distraction.

Morris Motors'
production line at
Cowley as Ken saw
it on a visit as a
child in the 1930s.
By 1935 output at
Cowley reached
10,000 cars a month

Yes, I had been living in a dream world. But it was a dream that I shared with nearly all of my contemporaries, of a new world that would be made better and happier by the internal combustion engine, and above all by the forthcoming increase in private cars. The same sorts of emotions and arguments are raised by the present-day prospect of almost unlimited growth in air travel – and the same sorts of doubts.

Popular With Ladies.

Illustrated:
AUSTIN 7 h.p. Fabric
Saloon .... £130.

There are two very good reasons why all Austin Cars are popular with ladies.

They are appreciative of the Austin's smart appearance and inviting interior . . . . pleased at the Austin's small refinements which show a careful attention to detail.

When they take the wheel themselves, the Austin's easy controls and finger-light steering are of exceptional appeal . . . . as is also the car's reputation for lastingly trouble-free running with the minimum of maintenance.

A third reason—and no less important! Austin offers the most complete range of cars made by any manufacturer in the world, which makes it possible for every household budget to include all the advantages of motoring at exactly the right cost.

In the 1930s, Austin and Ford introduced cheap family cars, even targeting ladies in their adverts. At £130, though, the Austin 7 cost more than a quarter of a senior teacher's annual salary

And what of the Mews? Its post-war history is almost worthy of words by Marx to music by Berlioz. Compulsorily purchased at the end of the 1960s, this late and transient symbol of the ascendancy of the horse, which my father converted to meet the needs of the age of petrol, was razed to the ground along with the surrounding area. In its place there arose a mighty monument to the triumph of the motor car – a multi-storey car park so huge and hideous that it roused many of the citizens to fury. Conservationists managed to get the top storey lopped off, but they could not stop it from being built. Sitting on its haunches (for on two sides its lines were at an angle to the horizontal), for over thirty years this Gorgon dominated the view of the city from St George's Terrace and many another point. All sorts of suggestions were made about how to hide its ugliness: the Automobile Association, for instance, urged that it should be covered with creeper, to form a sort of hanging gardens of Canterbury. At least one unfortunate motorist burst through its concrete sides, before at last it was demolished in 2002 to make way for a new shopping area in which there are only 500 car parking spaces, far fewer than in the multi-storey park. Most of those who come by car now park on the perimeter and travel in and out by bus. Rise from the grave, dear Mr Cox, and observe that your prophetic advice has at last been heeded!

4

A City of Shopkeepers

IT IS A myth that Napoleon described England as 'a nation of shopkeepers', but seventy years ago that phrase was lodged immovably in the public mind, because it was so obviously true. In Canterbury, as elsewhere, there was no necessity to 'go down the town' to do one's shopping, for there were usually shops much closer at hand. The smaller ones were often converted residences, sometimes in the most unexpected places such as the baker's that operated in a narrow street of terraced cottages in York Road, spreading an appetising but inescapable aroma to the entire neighbourhood. The housewives of Dover Street, having completed the essential morning ritual of whitening their doorsteps, could dart across the street, still in their slippers, to get their milk jug replenished at Mr Kennett's dairy. In that same street a couple of 'general stores', offering a limited range of provisions along with much else, vied with a 'real' grocer's shop where a gleaming bacon-slicing machine stood on the counter as evidence of the owner's specialist skills as a provision merchant, while the other needs of mankind and womankind were met by establishments, all originally built as dwellings, offering fuel, drapery and haberdashery, chimney sweeping, repairing of shoes and bicycles, saddlery and even jewellery and watchmaking. All these have long since disappeared, their plate-glass windows now curtained or diminished to domestic scale. Only the areas inhabited by the 'better people' (as the novelist Hugh Walpole coyly described the more prosperous citizens) were immune from the contamination of retail trade. One such was South Canterbury, but even there a thin crust of commerce had formed in the shape of a fruiterer's in Old Dover Road, perilously situated right at the edge of the carriageway, leaving no room for any pavement, and Mr Gann's cavernous, old-established grocer's shop in Lansdown Road.

The city was peppered with shops in a way that people of today would find hard to credit or understand. But this was only the most obvious way in which shopping then was something utterly different from shopping now. For a child growing up in that era, going to the shops was part of the business of learning how society worked. From an early age, I realized that the few shops that opened on Sundays were out of bounds to any right-thinking person, and particularly to children. This was unfortunate, as with a nice sense of strategy Satan had planted one of his outposts, a small sweetshop which sold a particularly delicious kind of lemonade powder that had a fizzy taste even when eaten raw, right at the foot of St George's Terrace where it joined Watling Street. This was only a hundred yards from our Sunday School in my Watling Street Congregational Church, so that although I never succumbed to temptation, I was keenly conscious of being between the poles of a moral magnet.

A little later I became aware that there was one sort of shop that my parents never patronized. These were the 'company shops', large and flourishing with prominent fascia boards bearing impressive titles such as 'International' or 'Home and Colonial'. All of them proclaimed in their windows – and the International also in regular display advertisements in the local press – the great advantage that they had over their rivals: low prices owing to their ability to buy in bulk. What they did not say was that these low prices were now due to another factor as well, their use of road transport to supply their stores direct instead of going through the established wholesalers such as Reynolds in Orange Street or Cox & Scott in Station Road West. Early in the 1930s, complaints were already being made in Council meetings about the traffic congestion in the main street being caused by the company shops' delivery lorries.

My parents' objections to these shops were based mainly on the idea that they were a threat to the independent local trader – a class to which we ourselves undoubtedly belonged. And of course they were right: most of the company shops prospered and gradually won a commanding position, until a generation ago they met the overwhelming competition of the supermarkets. My father's standpoint was a natural one for him to take, for on resigning his post of commanding officer of the Salvation Army corps in Canterbury in 1907, he had set up in business on his own, running some sort of a general store on an initial capital of only £10. Yet by the time I was born twelve years later, his business had grown to the point where he was supplying perhaps a quarter of the city's needs for household fuel. His lack of ready capital drove him to take on directors who were a financial help but a managerial encumbrance. Even so, he must have felt a good deal of satisfaction, as he turned fifty in the early 1920s, at what he had achieved despite his late start as a tradesman. In his early days he had earnestly studied two texts, the Bible and a Victorian best-seller, *Self Help*, by Samuel Smiles. When he quoted (as he often did) the text 'God helps those who help themselves', I leapt to the erroneous conclusion that it was from the Bible. He wanted the modest success that he had achieved, against the odds, to be widely available, and he was against the company shops because they seemed to put barriers across the self-help path that he had trodden.

Such scruples, however, did not seem to trouble my grandmother. Going shopping with her was a rare but special treat. Her regular grocer was the decidedly up-market firm of Theobalds and Cooper in the Buttermarket, just opposite Christ Church Gate to the Cathedral and the Precincts. There I was able to observe how her ready flow of banter had already established her as a 'character'. But she felt free to explore the company shops too, and in particular she seemed to favour the Maypole. This was a company shop, but its premises were quite small as it seemed to specialize

Theobalds & Cooper, a decidedly up-market grocer in the Buttermarket, was well patronized by Ken's grandmother. His father, a self-made man, supported these family shops against the growing power of what later became known as chain stores

in butter and cheese, to the exclusion of other sorts of groceries. Behind its counter there were masters of one of the many lost arts of retail trade. Using little wooden bats, they dug into immense heaps of butter and quickly shaped up the required amount into a beautifully symmetrical shape with fluted sides and the imprint of a clover leaf on the top. Weighed on the scales, each of these products performed perfectly, not needing a smear added or deducted to achieve the correct weight – or so it seems in the indulgent, amber-tinted glass of memory.

For us, therefore, there was no question of becoming customers of the company shops. All our groceries came from a shop on the corner of Lower Bridge Street and Church Street St Paul's, known as Brown's Stores. Bald-headed and avuncular, Mr Brown was always in attendance behind the brass scales that gleamed on the counter of the dusky interior. Along the front of that counter there was a sort of defensive barricade consisting of a row of biscuit tins with glass tops, from which Mr Brown could be relied on to extract one or two samples for a child of a regular customer. My mother certainly qualified for that description, for she did not pay cash but had her purchases 'entered', for payment weekly or monthly, in a little stiff-covered book embossed in gold with the name and address of Brown's Stores and with a celluloid-covered panel through which the hand-written 'Mrs Pinnock' could be seen.

One of the everyday necessities of any household was a shopping basket – or preferably, at least two. The first would be a strong, hand-crafted container made of wicker. There was a blind man, Mr Nason, whom I used to see as I passed his yard at the end of Old Dover Road, always at work deftly weaving the pliable strands that would later become as hard as wood. The second might be quite different, a soft bag, flat and almost triangular, of plaited rushes. This sort of bag was generally reserved for fish, but Sir John Betjeman, in his latter days as Poet Laureate, gave it a last lease of life as, with his battered hat, it was part of his regular uniform when he turned up to record television programmes – though I don't think he ever allowed it to appear on screen.

The simple objects of everyday life – shoes and shoe polish, the contents of a dressing table or bathroom cabinet – all have a host of things to tell us about the age to which they belong, if only we will quietly interrogate them and allow them to speak. This is undoubtedly true of baskets. How and why did the ladies of South Canterbury never carry one? The answer, according to the widow of one of the city's most prominent solicitors, was that when she and her friends went shopping, they would always ask for their purchases to be 'sent' – that is, delivered by bicycle or van through the garden gate, which bore a little porcelain plaque inscribed 'Tradesmen's entrance'. If a basket was to be found in their households, it was for the maidservant's use.

Apart from its significance as a class symbol, the basket can be viewed from the point of view of utility. Capacious as they might be, shopping baskets could never approach the weight and size of the contents of even a half-filled supermarket trolley of today. How did families feed themselves, armed with such poor means of transporting their needs? The answer is to be found partly in the battalions of tradesmen's bicycles, each with a large basket mounted on its handlebars, and increasingly – from the beginning of the 1930s – in the little vans scurrying everywhere. But mainly the answer is that at a time when refrigerators were only just appearing, and freezers unknown, frequent trips had to be made to the local shops. From time to time, too, there were lusty-voiced itinerant traders patrolling the suburban streets. A girl who grew up in York Road in the 1920s recalled how one of the 'fish men' used to sing out:

> *Fresh shrimps today*
> *from Whitstable Bay.*
> *What I don't sell*
> *I give away.*

The shopping basket can therefore be seen as an integral part of a pattern of shopping that has almost completely passed away. In its heyday, it had interesting social consequences. With their daily needs catered for almost on their doorsteps, many of the suburbs had something of a village atmosphere and developed a corresponding sense of identity. Most of the people of the populous Wincheap area did most of their weekly shopping at Bear's store, which was appropriately housed in the old manor house, while the rest went to Fagg's corner shop which was at the foot of a rise still known to local people as 'Fagg's Hill'. Recognizing that there was a distinct body of consumers who did not relish the trek to the main street, one of the 'chains', the British and Argentine Meat Company, set up shop near to Bear's. Commerce bred community: neighbours got to know each other better as they foraged for food, or dived into Mr E. P. D. Bush's chemist's shop for a bottle of his locally renowned Influenza Mixture. At carnival time, Wincheap people got together to make their own entry: one year it was 'The Mayor and Corporation of Wincheap', with the 'Mayor' riding precariously in a soap-box carriage.

How quickly and completely that pattern has faded, in keeping with the society that distinguished between those who would and those who wouldn't carry a basket. A few years ago, I had my last glimpse of the lady who described how as a youngster she would never have used a basket – she was in a supermarket, pushing a trolley!

Having delivered my sermon on the social significance of shopping baskets in the long-gone age of eighty years ago, I return to Mr Brown's store where my mother stands at the counter gripping the handle of one of those objects. What does she buy? First of all, ingredients for cake making: dried fruit of various sorts, crystallized peel with large remnants of sugar attached which I view with anticipation, rice for making puddings, which I hate, for in our household it is never used for anything of a savoury kind. Every one of these ingredients is shovelled out in Mr Brown's gleaming brass scoop into the pan of his massive scales, and from there deposited on a sheet of stiff blue paper which he deftly forms into a cone, its bottom screwed tight and the open ends securely folded over. They might have been even more secure if fastened with Sellotape, but there was then no such thing, only a rather new invention called 'Gumstrip', a brown tape that had to be licked to make it stick, and no one suggested that Mr Brown should do that. Tea and coffee beans, no less than the other items, might be scooped out of the great black japanned canisters, some marked with Chinese letters in gold and others marked 'Assam', 'Darjeeling' or 'Ceylon' which lined the wall behind the counter, but my mother ignored these antiquities because she had a settled policy of buying only Lyons's 'Green Label' tea. At seven pence halfpenny a quarter, this was the second best in the range of Lyons's teas; only the Red Label was superior. This, and hardly anything else, came prepacked by the manufacturer, bearing the assurance implied by a brand name. Unmoved by the little Brooke Bond red vans everywhere to be seen in the streets, she showed no inclination to experiment with their product, just as she was indifferent to the enormous advertisement hoarding that covered the entire façade of the building facing down Palace Street which showed an old lady sharing cups of Mazawattee tea with a little girl who could safely be assumed to be her granddaughter. Shopping was replenishment rather than experiment, a chore rather than recreation.

But for a child it was a voyage of discovery, and even for adults it could sometimes offer moments of elation. As I emerged from Brown's Stores clutching my complimentary biscuits in their paper bag (a plain one, not decorated with the shopkeeper's name in the florid copper-plate that most of his competitors favoured), I had a sense of being an actor in a drama. I had seen how adults comported themselves when they went shopping, how shopkeepers interpreted the 'civility' they all claimed as the distinguishing mark of their profession; and somehow the image of Mr Brown gained a romantic lustre as it merged in my mind with that of his transatlantic counterpart, Mr Hobbs, the grocer in *Little Lord Fauntleroy* which – though I soon learned never to reveal to my friends that I had even heard of such a book – was a prized Christmas present from my grandma.

As yet, my mother's basket was no more than three-quarters full. Much of the contents consisted of the cones formed on the counter which were used even for dangerously spillable things such as sugar. Indeed, a generation of primary schoolteachers took to using quantities of the stuff for artwork, still calling it 'sugar paper' long after it had disappeared from grocers' shops. The heavier items such as the cooking salt, a rectangular slab enclosed in a printed brown wrapper, or the bag of 'Seraflo' self-raising flour, would be delivered, along with the 'Hustler' soap whose wrappings we would strip off in order to cut out the coupons which, after many months of 'saving them up', would be sent off to claim a free gift. Such opportunities were then rare: the only other one I recall was a cardboard 'Ivory Castle', a cut-out toy awarded to regular users of Gibbs' Dentifrice, which dramatically presented in its artwork the need to use that product to fight the demon of dental decay.

The best part of the day's shopping was still to come. From Brown's Stores we walked down Broad Street, which despite its name was then little more than a lane, for the Star Brewery had been built against the city wall and then spread across part of the old carriageway, creating a bottleneck for traffic which persisted until 1931. Emerging from this lane to a part of the street that could honestly be called 'broad', we saw ahead of us, on the corner of Havelock Street, a little shop that was our goal – Bob Tolhurst, the butcher. There we would often meet my grandmother, I suppose by some prior arrangement, for she and her daughter were of one mind about Bob: he was the best butcher in town.

It was not, I think, just the quality of his meat that drew my grandmother, but equally her relish for Bob's personality, his endless stream of talk and the salty exchanges that it provoked. His shop was so tiny that it could take no more than four customers at a time, or five at the most, and all of them had to take care not to move too far backwards from his great chopping block, or they would find their clothes greased by the carcasses hanging in a row behind them. But when Bob had even as few customers as two, he had something more that was dear to his heart – an audience.

His hearers could count on receiving a lecture that was always the same as to its subject matter, but different in detail each time he delivered it. It was invariably about meat – how it should be reared, slaughtered and hung, and sometimes (though only rarely because it went without saying) with an appendix on the need for a butcher to be properly trained.

'You sin them pictures of the 'ooman anatomy,' he would say, 'You know, all them various veins and the like.' From this introduction he would rapidly progress to the other aspects of his syllabus, always laying special stress on the importance of hanging, sometimes dropping dark hints about the malpractices of some of his unnamed rivals who were in too much of a hurry to convert carcasses into cash. He spoke with authority, for he had his own slaughterhouse in his backyard and was therefore in charge of every stage of the entire process, from buying his cattle at the market to handing over the joints neatly wrapped in grease-proof with an outer covering of newspaper.

Bob's latter days were sad. Increasingly stringent public health regulations made it impossible for small individual butchers each to have their own slaughterhouse. To Bob, the prospect of becoming merely the dissector and distributor of other people's meat must have been intolerable. He put up his shutters for good, and for a long time the premises looked rather like an abandoned fortress. I heard he had become a jobbing gardener, and from time to time I would see him disconsolately wheeling a bike: surely this woefully diminished figure could not be the same Bob whose block had been his pulpit and his customers his congregation. His life's end came before his death; his shop has long since been converted into a house, but on its back gate there is still a ghostly reminder of him, for it is inscribed 'The Old Slaughterhouse'.

From Bob I got a vivid glimpse of how personal the relationship between shopkeeper and customer often – or even usually – was. Within the ambit of their craft, they found opportunities to express themselves, to acquire an individual face; the act of buying and selling was something more than an economic interchange. Later in life I was to see this in even more distinct detail in my father's office: how certain customers would insist on dealing with him personally, always claiming his attention and sometimes being invited into his inner office to choose a cigar from the box of Havanas that came to him, a life-long non-smoker, each Christmas; how others would pour out a long story of their personal woes, which he listened to with unfailing patience; how yet others, down on their luck, would be quietly interrogated and their character assessed (always with a good look at the state of polish of their boots, which my father considered a sure indicator of character or the lack of it), sometimes leaving with half a crown in their pockets and occasionally being offered the job of distributing handbills or individual accounts that otherwise would have gone in the post.

Perhaps the most striking example of all of the importance of personality in making a success of shopkeeping occurred soon after the end of the Second World War. In 1945–6 I worked for a spell in my father's office in Dover Street, and during that time I became aware that a young man named Bert Woods had exchanged his demob suit for warehouseman's overalls and opened a little shop further down the street. Quite soon I realized what an Aladdin's cave had come into existence. The shop was crammed with stock, all in apparent disarray, consisting of every kind of household article except food, but Bert and his wife knew exactly where to look to see if they had what they were asked for. Again and again, in other shops, I and others would be told, when inquiring for some elusive item, 'Sorry, but try Woods' Stores.'

In 1945, few could have foreseen how rapidly the prospects for small-scale shopkeeping would wane. Yet Bert Woods's shop went on and on for some forty years, and closed only when his health gave out. It became a Canterbury legend, to the extent that the local conservation society, the Oaten Hill Society, eventually acquired all its stock and presented it to the Museum of Canterbury, which has since put its remarkable collection of nearly or quite obsolete household articles on display. Sadly missing from the exhibit, however, was a video of Bert Woods at work, which would have revealed the mainspring of his success – the genuinely welcoming greeting, followed by the earnest attempt to understand and meet the customer's needs which, if successful, would lead to the usual parting words, 'Thank you for your custom.' An old-fashioned phrase, but this shopkeeper was one of the latest and best in a tradition that must go back centuries, to the shopkeepers of Becket's time whose identities, and even the precise locations of their premises, the historian William Urry was able to discover in the Cathedral's account books; and then to the Protestant refugees from France and the Low Countries whose descendants flourished mightily in both retail trade and manufacturing.

For many of the smaller tradesmen their own business was an arena large enough to absorb all their talents and energy. Some prospered, but others struggled, unable even to send their daughters to the Simon Langton School, according to one councillor in the early 1930s who inveighed against the high cost of education that the ratepayers had to shoulder. None the less, tradesmen of various kinds, from the single-handed tailor, Councillor Stone, to the leaders of the trading community such as Barrett, who combined philanthropy with the Midas touch which built up a fine business from scratch, Baynton, the secretary of the East Kent Road Car Company, Hooker, the mill-owner, and above all Lefevre, the presiding genius of the city's largest department store, played a major role in civic government. They devoted much time and energy to the Council, and shared their wealth with the community by generous gifts: wrought-iron gates for the Langton schools from Lefevre; Tower House and its splendid gardens from the Williamson tannery-owning family; and Larkey Valley woods from Hooker. These are only the outstanding examples of the spirit of benevolence that, incited by a blend of civic pride and evangelical religion, characterized significant numbers of the chief tradesmen and was shared with many of their lesser colleagues. Throughout its history, Canterbury had benefited from the generosity of its tradesmen, the most notable example being that of Alderman Simmons, 'Canterbury's Great Tycoon' as his biographer Frank Panton calls him, who gave the city its largest public park by landscaping the unkempt area of the Dane John early in the nineteenth century. The tradesmen-benefactors of the 1930s acted in the same tradition, but they were among the last of their kind: today the branch managers of nationwide supermarkets and stores, even if named on the till slips, are virtually anonymous, mere supervisors of the cash pipeline through which local spending flows to the centrally based management and thence to shareholders. Yet still an ironic vestige of the spirit that once animated local trade remains: look closely at your till slip and you will find on it a stilted paraphrase of Bert Woods's envoi – not 'Thank you for your custom,' but 'Thank you for shopping at Tesco [or wherever].'

Woods' Stores was a delight, and much of its appeal was that in this encumbered place his customers breathed the air of an age just gone by. It was a constant reminder, especially welcome to the many who prefer the familiar to the new, of the time when many of a town's shops were owned and managed by the people named on the fascia.

When I was ten or eleven, while we were still living on St George's Terrace only a few minutes' walk from the main street, I had a vivid glimpse of how quickly and utterly the distinctive character of a local business could be extinguished. Once past Woolworths and Pollard's, I would pause to have a good look at the shop window of Edwin Bing & Son, pharmaceutical chemists and perfumers, which announced its calling by displaying three enormous glass flagons of coloured water, the traditional symbol of the pharmacist, on a shelf near the top of the window. Glancing through the glass door, I would see Mr Bing or his assistant, Mr Rootes, hard at work preparing bottles of medicine. With its rich colours of fine wood, elegantly worked by cabinet makers into French-polished shelves and glass-topped display cases, it seemed a veritable temple of health. And so, surely, it was, for at the

Bing & Son were chemists, but the shop's pharmaceutical wares were permeated by the scent of its lavender toiletries, made from lavender grown at Grove Ferry

point where the two white-coated figures usually worked there was a Vestal flame, a slender jet of gas at which, as each bottle was wrapped in a sheet of pure white paper, a blob of sealing wax would be melted to fasten the package safely and secretly. From the few times when I had had good enough cause to venture inside, I knew well what incense I would smell: a delicate aroma of disinfectant mixed with lavender.

Yes, lavender, for this was the true glory of this shop, lifting it far above other 'chemists' shops' which merely dispensed medicines; for in the left-hand section of the window there was always on display a selection of the lavender-scented goods that the firm produced – soap, shaving soap, toilet waters in bewildering variety, all from the swampy fields adjoining the River Stour at Grove which were pictured and eloquently described. How I longed to go to Grove; and one day my wish was granted: soft winds brought gusts of the scent to me, and then there was the unexpected joy of crossing the tiny River Stour by ferry.

Yet all too soon this paradise was swept away, the lavender plantations torn up and replaced by nothing more interesting than turf for lawns and golf courses. This disaster was the sequel to an equally great one that in 1930 hit the shop in St George's Street. The firm of Edwin Bing sold out to a London company, Savory and Moore. Soon only the latter's products were on display, and the fine Victorian woodwork of the shopfront was replaced by an arty frontage that I didn't like. Worst of all, those great globes of glass, filled with liquids that somehow never seemed to evaporate, disappeared, retaining only a ghostly presence in stained-glass panels at the tops of the windows. The interior, too, was remodelled, according to the *Kentish Gazette*, though I disdained to enter and find out just what had happened. But through the door I could see just one point of continuity: Mr Bing was no longer there, but Mr Rootes, now evidently promoted to be manger of this alien enterprise, was still at his post.

Tragedies of this kind were to be enacted again and again as the company shops grew in strength: Bing's was the first, and therefore the most affecting, of those that I encountered; and in later decades, with the coming of the supermarkets, the wind of change grew to a hurricane. Yet in the 1930s there were still businesses enough of the old sort to mask the immensity and finality of the changes that were impending. Shopkeepers of the past whom my friend William Urry was discovering, such as Teric the Goldsmith and Simon the Mercer in the twelfth century, or the Puritan grocer's assistant, James Chilton, who played a leading part in organizing the sailing of the *Speedwell* and the *Mayflower* to New England in 1620, still had their counterparts in the 1930s – local people, known by name or in person to many citizens, active not only in their businesses but in every aspect of social and religious life.

When the Chamber of Trade held its annual meeting, its proceedings always took up almost a whole page of the local press, and the list of those attending seemed to contain nearly everyone who was anything in the city. Who could doubt that among the local tradesmen were to be found many of the pillars of local society? As I walked along St Margaret's Street, glancing through the glass door of the linen shop of A. H. Amey & Son I would see the impressive figure of Mr Amey, whom I knew not only as overlord of the 'best' shop of its kind in the city, but also as superintendent of the Sunday School at the Congregational church in Guildhall Street with which my own Sunday School joined forces twice a year. Behind the double-fronted eighteenth-century façade of the rather grand fruiterers and seedsmen, Taylor Brothers, you would find another masterful character, Herbert Taylor, dispensing packets of seeds which arrived by chute from the floor above, or lovingly caressing a real pineapple, a fruit still redolent of social superiority even though it was no longer available on hire, as in Victorian times, to grace a dinner table without any intention that it should actually be consumed. To me, however, Mr Taylor was a star performer at church concerts, where he performed the most amazing conjuring tricks to an incessant flow of witty 'patter'. Within a few yards of Miss Pierce's school was a little but very well-kept shop that displayed nothing more than a few bolts of cloth. Its owner, Councillor Stone, did not believe in advertisements, disdaining capitals on his fascia board and substituting only his not very legible signature in gold leaf on a dark green background. It was quite enough, for everyone knew that this was his home, and his tailoring establishment, from which he ventured to do battle in the Council chamber, a mere five minutes' walk away, with his arch rival in debate, Alderman Barrett.

Barrett himself was deservedly one of the best-known Canterbury figures of his generation, as benefactor to the city, elder statesman and, above all, successful businessman. Much the same could be said of some others, notably Charles Lefevre, the owner and guiding spirit of the town's principal department store, a short, stubby figure whose Huguenot origins were obvious from his appearance no less than his name, a man of immense energy which he drained to the last dregs when war came, or Hooker, whose gift of Larkey Valley, marked by a millstone, is an enduring symbol of that public-spirited era. To me, as I read the papers or listened to discus-

Lefevre was Canterbury's principal department store during the inter-war period. William Lefevre, whose name provided a link with the Huguenot refugees of the seventeenth century, was a leading light of contemporary society

sions from the late 1920s onwards, these and many others I have not mentioned were great figures.

Barretts of Canterbury survives today as a dealer of 'prestige' cars, yet few of the other great names of that time are now to be seen on the city's shops or in advertisements. Their day was coming to an end. Winds of change were sweeping through the shopping streets, and the sort of transformation that I witnessed at Bing's would be continually repeated.

5

Print

WE LIVED IN a print-based society – there could be no doubt about that. I knew it long before I could ever have found the words to express it. Print was the source of all knowledge and news, and most of our entertainment. Every weekday the *Daily Mirror* plopped through our letter box, and once a week there was also the *Sunday Companion*. Scruples of conscience prevented my father from buying a Sunday paper, but not from accepting the *Sunday Express* when he visited his foreman late on Sunday evening to plan the next day's work. As infants, my brother Ron and I drank in the adventures of the Bruin Boys family in the *Rainbow* or *Tiger Tim's Weekly*, with lovely colour illustrations, but as we grew older these full-colour weeklies were replaced by cheaper 'comics' such as *Film Weekly*, costing only a penny but printed in black on tinted paper. These strip-cartoons, all featuring famous stars of the silent screen such as Harold Lloyd, had to come out of our threepence a week pocket money, but my father tried to divert our thoughts into more serious channels by providing us with the *Children's Newspaper*, which was edited by an earnest and indefatigable character called Arthur Mee.

'The *Daily Mail* is for people who can't think and the *Daily Mirror* is for those who can't read,' my father told us with a smile. But he made no apology about being a *Mirror* reader – very sensibly, he claimed that it gave him the main news in a nutshell and therefore equipped him to meet customers who would undoubtedly raise issues of the day.

There came a moment in 1926 when for several days the only newspaper to arrive was a government handout called the *National Gazette*, and I can see now my father sitting at the breakfast table under the gaslight, turning over the skimpy pages with disgust – not because he sympathized with the strikers, but because he had been deprived of an essential ingredient of his daily diet of information.

I soon realized that my father's remark (no doubt not his own invention, but something he had heard or read) about the *Mirror* being for non-readers was just a joke. In fact, the paper contained a lot of solid print, even a serial story that took up a whole page, which was of no interest to Ron and me. But near the end of its thirty-two pages there was sheer enchantment – the strip-cartoon adventures of Pip, Squeak and Wilfred, a dog, a penguin and a

Ken and his brother were captivated by the Pip, Squeak and Wilfred strip cartoons in the Daily Mirror

rabbit who rapidly assumed reality in our minds. This was the *Mirror*'s answer to the Rupert Bear feature in the *Daily Express* which had been created by the Canterbury-born artist, Mary Tourtel, and to other similar circulation-building features such as J. F. Horrabin's strip-cartoons of Japhet and the Arkcubs in the *News Chronicle*. What we did not realize was that the chummy letters to young readers of the *Mirror* from 'Your affectionate Uncle Dick' were a local product, for Uncle Dick was Mr E. J. Lamb, who lived at Whitstable, and A. B. Payne, the artist who drew the Pip, Squeak and Wilfred strips, lived at Herne Bay.

In all this mass of ephemeral print one strand is clearly detectable – an effort at social conditioning. In the *Children's Newspaper* this was quite blatant. We were continually urged not to become 'litter louts' – so that in adult life I winced if I saw a youngster toss a discarded drinks can on the pavement. A prolific author of guidebooks and editor of the *Children's Encyclopaedia*, Arthur Mee had much to say about saving the environment – he particularly approved of a petrol filling station that had put little thatched roofs over its pumps. The Arkcubs' lifestyle seemed to echo the liberal values of the *News Chronicle*, but a political slant of a different kind sometimes crept into the *Mirror*'s children's pages, for among the benign and almost-human animals created by A. B. Payne we occasionally saw a sinister, bearded figure called Wyzovski – obviously a Russian terrorist – who was always carrying a smoking bomb. The *Sunday Companion* was of course specifically designed to provide pious reading-matter in a digestible form, so although it always contained a printed sermon – and I always felt something of a glow of local pride when it was by our local Baptist minister, the Reverend Allan M. Ritchie – there were two serial stories which seemed to me to follow a pretty set pattern (so far as I could judge from cursory scanning). This consisted of the heroine becoming really interested in the new curate by the second instalment and arriving at the altar at the conclusion. It was all in black and white, of course, with few illustrations, but from time to time there was the bonus of a full-colour pictorial insert of a sunset over the sea or a poppy-strewn landscape – anything that had plenty of red in it.

Underlying almost everything we read in newspapers or magazines was a profound bias in favour of the existing order in politics, religion and indeed the structure of society. In form and content, these pages of print reflected the ideas and ideals of the dominant middle class. Yet change was in the air: the 'common people' had begun to cast off deference and demand something more in keeping with their own background and tastes. Newspapers of a new sort, owing much to the influence of popular magazines such as *Answers* and *Tit-Bits*, found a ready market. They were no longer broadsheets with acres of solid print, but tabloid-sized, full of pictures and even cartoons, still with plenty of 'news' but concisely presented. The broadsheets, led by *The Times*, the *Daily Telegraph* and the *Morning Post*, went on much as before, in lofty unawareness that one day, far ahead in the future, even they would have to imitate the tabloids in many ways as the price of survival. Among the rest of the national papers, there were bitter circulation wars. The *Daily Herald* offered cheap sets of the works of Dickens and H. G. Wells to regular readers. I often saw these books, bound distinctively in imitation leather, on my friends' shelves, and as other offshoots of these circulation wars there were free entertainments on the Dane John, community singing sessions organized by the *News Chronicle*, and performances by the *Daily Mirror*'s 'thirty-two pages' – a troupe of boy gymnasts in page-boy uniforms.

As a daily student of the *Mirror*, around 1930 I thought I detected a new stage in this battle for circulation. It seemed to me that there was a distinct change of climate: the solid feature articles (such as one by Russell Pasha on the international drugs trade) disappeared, the society-based chitchat was replaced by a hard-hitting columnist called 'Cassandra' (the pen name of William N. Connor) who used the language of the common man with tremendous eloquence, and there was even a new feature,

'Jane's Journal', which was in every sense of the word a 'strip'-cartoon. My parents survived this tidal wave of change, but not without a struggle, and eventually in the early 1940s my mother chose to have her own daily paper, the *News Chronicle*, which was surely one of the most civilized popular newspapers in our history.

What effect did all this change, of which the *Daily Mirror* was only one element, have on the local press in Canterbury? The answer is, very little. The standard format was the large page of the old-established national dailies; the style of presentation and the contents were local variants of these august models. They were essentially 'newspapers of record', setting out local events not as 'stories' (to use the current term) but as factual reports. In a city of some 25,000 inhabitants, with a rural hinterland of perhaps 15,000 more, there were no fewer than four local newspapers: the *Kentish Observer* and the *Kentish Express* on Tuesday, the *Kent Herald* on Wednesday, and the *Kentish Gazette* on Friday; and there was even, for a short time, a local evening paper, the *Evening Echo*. It was exciting to hear its name shouted by a newsboy near its offices in St Margaret's Street – but it soon folded.

What the readers of local newspapers wanted most of all was detail. Week by week the farming community could rely on finding the latest market prices for livestock and produce, including hops and what was called 'London hay and straw', and special attention was given to vegetables and fruit, for that was a time when a village like Wingham would be embowered every spring amid many blossom-laden acres. My grandmother always turned first to the list of what she called 'hatches, matches and dispatches', a feature strangely missing from present-day local newspapers, except in the unsatisfactory form of paid-for advertisements. Any of these events that related to prominent members of the trading community were treated very fully, with lists of donors of presents, from a butter knife upwards, or the names of those attending a funeral, taking up many column inches. The organist at a funeral, and the hymns he played, might well get a mention, but the appetite for detail was not quite what it had once been: no longer did the reporters feel bound to transcribe the messages written on the wreath-cards, as in some Folkestone local papers of the 1880s that I have seen.

Above all, this passion for detail expressed itself, as I shall try to show under the heading 'CCBC', in the reports of the monthly Full Council meetings and the committees that followed it. But almost equally, full coverage was given to court proceedings, both those in the Guildhall, where the Mayor presided following ancient custom, or the more august Quarter Sessions in Longport. These reports began with the name of the presiding judge, followed by the bench of magistrates, who were listed in anything but alphabetical order. First came the only woman, then the only man with a title ('Sir'), followed by six men with military rank (Colonel, Major or Captain – two of each), and finally thirteen civilians who were all merely 'Mr'.

Quarter Sessions produced moments of real drama. There was one week when the *Kentish Gazette* was nowhere to be seen in our household. After an extensive search I found it stuffed under a settee. My mother should have known that it was a very unsatisfactory hiding place in which to conceal it from an inquisitive twelve-year-old. It gave a full account of the trial of a former Sheriff of the city who was accused of harbouring a young girl from Northgate at his home in South Canterbury. It was a case that had already aroused intense local interest, causing long queues to form outside the Guildhall when the preliminary hearing was held. For the Quarter Sessions trial, the defendant engaged one of the most eminent lawyers of the day. It was easy enough to grasp from the press reports the sense of awe that Sir Henry Curtis Bennett inspired, but even he was able to do no more than advance pleas of mitigation. When the sentence of two months' hard labour was pronounced, the defendant's estranged wife fell in a dead faint.

The reports of the lesser courts were inevitably far more humdrum. Yet they had qualities that give them lasting value, for they preserve the precise turns of speech that humble and inarticulate people of that age actually used. They tell us how a tramp, who had stolen some chickens on Christmas Eve, reacted when he was arrested; and how a fourteen-year-old illiterate boy and his parents – all described as 'travellers' – tried to explain how and why the boy had stolen money from an unoccupied house. As a policeman approaches, the tramp exclaims, 'Somebody has put the wheeze on you', and when asked to explain why several car-casses were stuffed under his clothing, he says, not untruthfully, 'I wanted them for someone who was hungry.' The young boy is asked in the juvenile court if he had realized that what he had stolen was a hospital collecting box, and he replies that he can neither read nor write. Fining the boy (and effectively his parents) ten shillings, the chairman of the magistrates speaks his mind. He tells the parents that it is disgraceful, 'in these days of free educa-tion', that their son is illiterate. Likewise, the chairman of the six magistrates sitting in the main court says to the tramp, as he sen-tences him to two months' hard labour, 'there is nothing more irritating to persons who keep and feed fowls than to have persons like the prisoner come to steal them and wring their necks'. Throughout there is an unmistakable sense that the actual words of all the participants, even the magistrates' fatuities, have been faithfully reproduced. The eminent scholar M. R. James, who wrote some of the best ghost stories in the English language, found some of his favourite reading in the reports of English trials – surely because they, like the local newspaper reports, give direct access to the speech of the silent majority.

Embedded in some of these court reports are affecting stories of real life. There is the postmaster of the township of Lydd on Romney Marsh, for instance. He has an unprofitable stationery business alongside the post office, he pays an assistant thirty shillings a week, his business is clearly failing, and he milks his takings to the extent of about £129. That is the beginning of his downfall; he gets into the hands of moneylenders – 'vampires', he calls them. He has an impressive record of public service as a special constable and a volunteer member of the local fire brigade which the judge does not fail to mention before he describes this as 'a very serious case', of which 'an example must be made'. Then he pronounces sentence: six months in the second division. Like so much else in the paper, this report offers a lesson in citizenship, a reminder of how heavily the hand of the law could fall on any who succumbed to temptation.

Avidly though the national newspapers were read, they were not always trusted to tell the truth. More than once I had to endure the scornful put-down of 'Surely you don't believe everything you read in the papers'; and when I went to a public debate in the Central Cinema about the Spanish Civil War, I heard roars of laughter from the audience as one speaker introduced the names of two of the most prominent press barons into his speech:

> *If we would keep the stream of knowledge*
> *running pure and clear*
> *We first must stem the Beaverbrook*
> *and dam the Rothermere.*

Later on, with equal effect, he capped this with Humbert Wolfe's lines:

> *Thank God you cannot bribe or twist*
> *The honest British journalist*
> *But considering what the chap'll do*
> *Unbribed there's no occasion to.*

Were the local papers viewed with equal cynicism? I think not. No doubt their editors and proprietors must sometimes have been under pressure from people who wanted something to be 'kept out of the papers'. Did any of them succumb? The fact that there were five of them (or effectively four, after the *Kent Herald* joined forces with the *Kentish Gazette* in the 1930s), all competing in the same field, was a safeguard. Perhaps one of the local papers might have revealed – though as far as I know none ever did – that our local MP, Sir William Wayland, who kept the House of Commons in fits when he ridiculed a proposal to introduce American-style Prohibition in England, and who campaigned constantly for a reduction in the tax on 'the working man's pint', had a regular job in addition to being an MP – as analytical chemist to a brewery. But what happened to a bishop when he tried, for quite innocent reasons, to gag the local press, points I think to the truth of this matter.

Reports of dinners, which go completely unnoticed nowadays, were staple ingredients of the local papers of that time. The reporters sat in a group, apart from the diners but within easy earshot of the speakers. Sometimes their table was covered with green baize, but if they were more fortunate it had a white table-cloth suitably furnished for them to share the meal. The Bishop of Dover, Alfred Rose, liked dining out, and as he was an excellent speaker, he was frequently invited. On one occasion he prefaced his speech with, 'Look here, you chaps, please don't report what I say tonight, because I have to go to another dinner on Friday and I want to use the same material.'

Not even for a bishop would the assembled reporters collude in the gagging of the press. It was a difficult situation, but they found the answer. When the Bishop opened his *Kentish Gazette* the following Friday, he read with some dismay a report of the event that ended, 'The Bishop then told some exceedingly entertaining anecdotes which we regret we are not at liberty to print.' He soon realized that honour had been preserved on all sides: the gentlemen of the press had made their point, and he had added one more shaft to his quiverful of after-dinner stories.

Local newspapers, like almost every other aspect of society and the national newspapers, clearly reflected the dominance of the middle class. In form and content, they were what that class expected newspapers to be: papers of record in which one could quickly find the Council and court reports. Within the twelve pages of the *Kentish Gazette* there was room for these and much else besides. The letters to the Editor were relatively few, but often very long by present standards. In the early 1930s there was such a long and fierce battle between opponents and adherents of the Roman Catholic Church, arising from a campaign by the anti-Catholic followers of J. A. Kensit, the founder of the Protestant Truth Society, that eventually the editor of the *Kentish Gazette* took the unusual step of declaring the correspondence closed. But by the middle of the decade, there is a notable change. More and more it is international affairs that correspondents write about – the merits and evils of the various 'isms' that were competing for power and allegiance. In 1939, for instance, there is a long letter from one P. Whittam, writing from an address in St Alphege Lane which was the weekend retreat of Sir Oswald Mosley, the leader of the British Union of Fascists, trying to explain the Nazis' mis-treatment of German Jews, with an equally substantial response from the Canterbury-born artist William Townsend, some of whose pictures now hang in the gallery of the Royal Museum. About the same time there is a series of articles about the history of the streets of Canterbury, foreshadowing even longer articles that were to come from William Urry in the 1950s about the Pilgrim Fathers and their connections with Canterbury. All of these were of a nature and length that would be unthinkable in newspapers of today.

Only in the *Kentish Observer* was there any attempt, so far as I know, to gain circulation by broadening the paper's appeal, but it did this in a manner that confirmed how deep-dyed the middle-class ethos was. This paper devoted most of one page to feature articles, clearly bought off the peg from some agency, that were aimed at women readers. One of these was called 'Mrs Pepys's Diary'. Written in a style that feebly and unsuccessfully tried to imitate Samuel Pepys's, it provided simple household hints, each with its farcical preamble such as 'Expecting Mr Pepys's Aunt Lettice to drink tea with me, to my kitchen to make a batch of small cakes from the following recipe.' Mrs Pepys has endless advice to offer, much of it concerned with laundry problems such as how to remove paint spots or wash coloured garments, but the height of absurdity is reached when she gives a recipe for 'Canterbury lamb' – that is, frozen meat from New Zealand.

Not one in a hundred, perhaps one in a thousand, of the readers of this feature would ever have dipped into *Pepys's Diary*. Why, then, this ridiculous wrapping for what could have been straight-forward household hints? One answer could be that domestic help was becoming more and more expensive. In the small advertisements columns of the 1920s there had been offers of jobs at pitiful wages, even as little as £19 a year for 'general household duties', but by the 1930s many housewives had become resigned to managing without domestic help. Housework, therefore, needed to be given the right image, one that would bear no taint of working-class drudgery.

Leaving aside this inept attempt to build circulation, the local papers of that time command respect and even admiration. Within the confines of the ruling concept of what a newspaper should be, they did a fine job. Lapses of grammar or spelling were extremely few, and one has only to read them to be convinced that the reporters of that time were true professionals. In some of his Sherlock Holmes stories, Conan Doyle introduces reports from local papers written in a turgid and prolix style. What his models for these were, I don't know, but the newspapers of my childhood were of a quite different kind.

No less impressive is the feat of organization that these papers called for. Council meetings ended late on Wednesday evenings. Within the next twenty-four hours, the report had to be written, set up in type, slotted into the space that had no doubt been left for it, and printed; and then the 5,000 copies of the *Kentish Gazette* had to be distributed to the newsagents in Canterbury and the numerous agents in the countryside. At the age of ten I had bought, by mail order through an advertisement in the *Daily Mirror*, a little printing machine called the Adana. It consisted simply of a hollowed-out block of wood into which the type was fitted, and on which an inking roller and a platen were mounted. But it used real type, the twenty-six soldiers of lead that since the time of Caxton (who, William Urry later told me, probably once lived in St Alphege Lane) had conquered the world. Having struggled myself to set and print a tiny amount of this type, I found myself wondering how the *Kentish Gazette* could work the miracle of telling us all on Friday morning what had gone on in the Council chamber on Wednesday evening.

The Beaney was the Royal Museum and Public Library. It owed its name – the one that everyone normally used – to the Honourable J. G. Beaney, a Canterbury boy who started his working life as a pharmacist's assistant and then made his fortune as a doctor in Australia by very dubious means. Returning to end his days in his native city, he decided to perpetuate his name by endowing an Institute for working men. This absorbed a considerable part of his fortune, and most of the remainder of his money was spent on a monumental tomb in the Cathedral so hideous that the Dean and Chapter worked out a new policy to prevent any recurrence of such a disaster. There was not enough money left, though, to prevent Beaney's sister from ending her days in the workhouse.

The City Council accepted Beaney's legacy but altered the basic concept, so that no special provision was made for education other than through museum exhibits and books, magazines and newspapers. Inside and out the Beaney was – and is – a remarkable creation. Its style was described as 'Renaissance', and it is in fact a fake Elizabethan building such as no architect living in the reign of Good Queen Bess would ever have dreamed of. Yet strangely, in the course of time it has become a period piece, a building that in every detail breathes the spirit of Imperial splendour of the year 1897 in which it opened. It is a monster that I gradually learned to love, and I find I am not alone in this sentiment.

Since the 1930s, inevitably the Beaney has been converted in some ways to new uses that have somewhat obscured the original layout, and even greater changes are about to take place. So I will describe how it was when, after hearing from a school friend about some side-splittingly funny stories about a schoolboy called

'William' that could be borrowed free from the Beaney, I sidled past the mangy stuffed lion standing guard at the top of its entrance steps. On the right there was a large and lofty room, with people queuing to enter at one of its doors and then filing out, with books in their hands, from the other door. Once inside, I saw the library staff hard at work, extracting a ticket from each book chosen by a reader and popping it into the reader's ticket (itself a pocket of just the right size and shape), and then filing away the pregnant pouches which, after a fortnight, would give birth to a warning postcard and a fine. This simple and effective system, I learned in due course, had been introduced only a few years previously; before that, readers had been denied a pleasure that I soon learned to relish enormously – the freedom to search, to dip and to discover. To begin with, I was shepherded into the 'Junior Library', an enclave formed by bookcases where I soon found that all the 'William' titles were invariably 'out' – the only consolation then being the chance to read the copies of *Pictorial Education* and the *Children's Newspaper* that were laid out on the tables. But after a few weeks of going to the library every weekday, so that I read *A Boy's Life of Mark Twain* twice from cover to cover, I was told that I could use the adult library despite the fact that I was two years under the statutory age of fourteen. From that day forward, the library became my first university.

If I could be transported back seventy-five years, I would be able to tell any reader just where to look in the library for the books on watercolours or collecting old silver, that books on the 'new' Freudian psychology were within hailing distance of William James's *Varieties of Religious Belief*, and that the long stripe of grey along the outer wall of the Junior Library was the collected works of Balzac, translated into English but never, so far as I could see, opened or even disturbed. But most eagerly of all, I would want to point out a bookcase near the great front windows that was worth looking at, not for the ancient volumes in *The Story of the Nations* series, but for the still crisp new books, which seemed to be added at the rate of at least one a month, on Soviet Russia. As early as

For the twelve-year-old Ken, the Beaney was a treasure house, and sparked off his lifetime fascination with books

1918, an American journalist had pronounced a judgement on the Soviet Union which became famous: 'I have seen the future, and it works.' But was that true? All these new books had that question at their core. Yes or no? For a long time I sat on the fence, but at last I was convinced by the show trials of engineers and other technocrats that the Soviet Union was a cruel despotism.

I quickly realized what a demand for books there was. There was always a crowd of borrowers round the central shelves where the just-returned books were dumped unsorted. Among these would be found the newest acquisitions, still freshly jacketed, the crime novels of Edgar Wallace, G. D. H. and Margaret Cole or Dorothy L. Sayers, or the latest novel by Daphne du Maurier. The thirst for reading matter was slaked not only by the Beaney's 600 books issued each day apart from Wednesday when there was early closing, but also by several 'twopenny libraries', offering books at twopence a week. It was to these that many of those seeking the romances of Nesta Pain or the tales of Warwick Deeping went if they could not find them in the Beaney's shelves and could not afford to take out subscriptions at Boots or Austen's stationery shop.

I began to see books as desirable objects in themselves, and I became a hunter of the city's secondhand bookshops, such as Mr Cheshire in St Alphege Lane or Mr Beasley in Burgate, or a strange old man in North Lane who wore khaki shorts in summer and seemed resentful rather than pleased whenever he sold one of his carefully catalogued stock. I was impressed, too, by the care the Beaney staff took to look after their stock. They had contracts with specialist repairers who picked books to pieces so that each section could be 'guarded' with new reinforcement before being re-cased in stout boards, often with leather spines lettered in gold. This work must have been very costly in time and money, but it kept in circulation many books that had long gone out of print. There were so many of these re-bound volumes, all dressed in much the same handsome but rather sombre uniform, that the library shelves of that time looked quite different from the brightly jacketed kaleidoscope of today.

The 'Free Library' proclaimed on the signboard above its main entrance was not all the Beaney had to offer. On the left of the entrance hall there was the 'Magazine Room'. Here there were rows of reading desks in facing pairs, separated by wide slots in which stood a wide range of periodicals, each in its gold-lettered stiff cover: the weeklies such as the *Spectator*, the *New Statesman*, *The Nation, Time and Tide* and *The Listener* and a host of others, some contributed and some bought by the library. This wonderfully equipped room was a perfect place for browsing, and it provided a counterpoint to the well-stocked library on the other side of the hall. Having read a number of booklets in the main library by a retired Indian Army officer expounding the idea of reincarnation, I discovered the same idea echoed in the pages of *The Theosophist*. I read on, and found some interesting experiments on the influence of the moon on the growth of crops such as potatoes. Then I came to an account by two ladies who had visited the Wagner festival at Bayreuth, where they had seen

Hitler himself in his box at the opera house. They observed his 'aura', the emanation invisible to the ordinary eye but not to their psychic vision; and they concluded their article by remarking how refined and spiritual Hitler's aura was compared with that of a butcher. That finished Theosophy for me: I simply could not credit that Hitler was a more advanced specimen of humanity than good old Bob Tolhurst.

The Beaney was indeed a temple of print. Its most populous place of worship was of course the lending library, but its Magazine and Newspaper Rooms were chapels of almost equal importance. The walls of the Newspaper Room were lined with great wooden desks, each surmounted by the name of the paper in gold on a varnished plaque, and each bearing a brass strip that held the paper fast. The room was really something like a public bar, with customers standing to drink in the news, for along the skirting ran a footrest, again of highly polished brass. All the national and local papers were there, including even *Moscow News* and its successor, the *Daily Worker*, the organ of the Communist Party in Britain. In a Council debate it was agreed to admit these Communist dailies, provided of course that they were donated and not bought. Councillor Stone argued strongly in favour, on the grounds that in a democracy all opinions should be heard. There was a widespread, and probably correct, view that the paper was paid for by Dean Hewlett Johnson. In due course, the *Daily Worker*, like all its contemporaries, had its own little plaque in letters of gold, a token of the City Fathers' belief that democracy was strong enough to withstand any assault.

As sixth-form pupils of the Langton, I and my best friend, Evan Hopton, were allowed to use one room in the Beaney for what was called 'private study', though in fact we spent much of that time in discussion about such things as Richard Crossman's new book, *Plato Today*. We sat there, enjoying peace and comfort of a kind totally lacking in the present-day Reference Library, blissfully unaware that, according to legend, the table had been stolen by a nineteenth-century Mayor from its rightful owner, whose name is (or then was) chalked on the underside. But we were aware of something more important than that. All around us were evidences of the supremacy of print: in the stacked shelves of the locked cases of that room, in the lending library, Magazine and Newspaper Rooms. We were at the quiet centre of an empire of print, whose supremacy could never be substantially challenged or diminished.

But we were wrong. Already there was one example of the immense power of science, in the shape of electronics, to provide information and entertainment, and eventually to shape society with a power comparable to that of print.

6

Waves

SOMETIMES WE CALLED it 'wireless' and at other times 'the wireless', but never 'the radio'. Although the BBC used that word in the title of *Radio Times*, it did not invade everyday speech until long after the start of broadcasting in the early 1920s. In my earliest years I quickly became aware that 'the wireless' was the wonder of the age. Yet for me that word was tinged with melancholy, for it brought back the recollection of the saddest event of my young life – the death of one of my closest friends.

Kenneth Miles lived at the far end of the Dane John in a handsome bow-fronted Regency house, the last one of a terrace. One day he stood beside me, silent but supportive, when I was challenged by a group of children to prove my assertion that, though only seven years old, I could read. Accordingly I declaimed the text written in fat italics on the notice board near one of the main gates, but when I came to the word 'prohibited' I stopped abruptly. Such a word could not really exist, I believed, even in the vocabulary of the Town Clerk, Mr Henry Fielding, whose name appeared at the foot of the board. It must be a mistake. So I substituted my own version, 'forbidden', only to be corrected by the eldest of my inquisitors. Derision and shame were heaped on my head; I not only had to admit that I had got it wrong, but I had to do so to a *girl*.

The events of that morning were against Nature, but Kenneth stood by me from first to last. I think he argued that what I had said was not a mistake, but deliberate. My opponents were unconvinced, but at least I felt that I was not alone in the world. After this, our friendship rapidly ripened. His father, he said, was the headmaster of a school in Whitstable whose great hobby was this mysterious thing called 'wireless'. And it *was* mysterious. If questioned, some of my more knowledgeable elders would have been able to tell me that 'wireless' was short for 'wireless telegraphy'. 'Telegraphy' was understandable enough, for everywhere along the roads and the railways the telegraph wires were strung high up – was their harmonious humming due to the wind, I wondered, or was it caused by the messages buzzing back and forth? But wireless telegraphy, making use of waves of energy whose existence most people had never suspected – that was something quite bewildering. It belonged to the world of fantasy – to the story of Peter Pan, or the magic carpets of the Arabian Nights that could provide instant aerial transport to anywhere in the world.

It was Kenneth who gave me a glimpse of this miracle, the first hint I had that here was something that was about to invade almost every home in the land. Wireless was then, in the mid-1920s, an absorbing hobby for enthusiasts rather than a medium of entertainment. One day when none of his elders was at home, greatly daring, Kenneth led me into the basement where his father's 'wireless room' was. I saw great tangles of connecting wires, tuning knobs and condensers, pairs of coils of wire mounted in such a way that they could be made to bow to each other and then straighten up, and in one corner a serpentine, black horn that evidently was there to emit sound if all this equipment was used successfully. Keenly aware that we were on forbidden ground, we stayed only a few moments for fear of discovery. I came away with a feeling of utter incomprehension, wondering how anyone could wish to spend his spare time on this dreary thing called 'wireless'. That it would ever play any part at all in my own life, never entered my mind.

Then for a while I neither heard nor saw anything of Kenneth, until one morning my cousin Daisy, who was in effect if not in name my nursemaid, woke me up and told me to sit on the bed before I started to get dressed. She had bad news to tell me, that Kenneth had died after having rheumatic fever. It was the worst moment of my young life and, by association, my sadness at losing my best friend fused with the memory of our last afternoon together when we crept into the 'wireless room'. Given the opportunity of choosing, I would have decided never to think about wireless again.

But I had no such choice. For a long while, my family showed no interest in the wireless, but it was impossible to ignore its existence. In addition to the established retailers such as Barretts and Gouldens, little 'radio shops' sprang up offering not only ready-made sets, but kits for home construction. There was Mr A. B. Godden in Oaten Hill, for instance, who proudly advertised a kit that involved no soldering; and in the small ads section of the local papers you could discover that young Mr Norman Rollason, of Wincheap, was offering to make you a set to your own specifications. That was the start of a business that lasted until his retirement some fifty years later, but for only a few years was there a market for new sets produced locally by such people as Mr S. W. Bligh, Norman Rollason or Mr A. B. Godden. Very soon the big manufacturers such as Pye, Cossor, Murphy and many others won a dominating position. Prices fell year by year, until towards the end of the 1930s, in our sixth-form economics lessons, our teacher, Cyril Ward, would cite wireless as the most obvious example of a commodity whose price fell as production and demand increased.

Wireless brought new opportunities to the city's tradesmen, including even my father, for from the mid-1920s onwards he sold and delivered large numbers of 'wireless poles' – the tall posts that sprang up like a forest in back gardens over the next twenty years. Archaeologists of the future will find a stratum of curious little porcelain objects, oval in shape and pierced by two holes. These were the insulators through which the parallel aerial wires were strung. Garages and other outlets advertised their readiness to charge up accumulators for twopence a volt; and soon it was common to see people carrying one of these rather fragile objects, made of glass and containing acid, in a strong metal case with a handle. Many also bought large dry batteries, for as late as 1935 one advertisement in the *Kentish Gazette* said that 'a big proportion' of the population of the Canterbury area had no mains electricity. Even if you were 'on the mains', there was the problem that the Corporation's supply was direct current, though a change to alternating current was said to be coming. For many, this dilemma was eventually solved by the introduction of sets that were both AC and DC.

It may have been these complications that deterred my father from ever thinking seriously about getting a wireless set, despite the growing volume of propaganda that my brother, Ron, and I voiced. All our friends, we complained, were talking about what they heard on the wireless, but we could take no part. My father, however, seemed to find all he needed of the day's news and comment in the national and local papers, and saw little reason why he should allow alien voices to mingle with those of the family. Moreover, we moved house as the 1930s began, and he had to repay a mortgage instead of paying a very modest rent. Wireless sets were still relatively expensive: despite the continually falling market, by 1935 the sets offered by the main retailer, Barretts, ranged from £5 to £17, at a time when the pound sterling was worth at least a hundred times as much as today.

It was Ron, however, who found the solution. He haunted the radio shops and had made a particular friend of Norman Rollason; and he was an avid reader of weeklies such as *Practical Wireless*, which were full of advice on home construction of wireless sets. These magazines continued to flourish despite the increasing emphasis on commercially made sets. Ron decided to make his own wireless, even winding the coils himself on a little Meccano gadget that sometimes had to be dislodged from the kitchen table so that we could sit down to lunch. What he eventually produced was far from elegant – just a baseboard on which

Home construction of wireless sets was popular

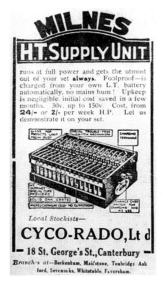

This is an advert for high-voltage power for radios

the tuning coils, condenser and a couple of valves were mounted, along with a mass of wiring neatly soldered together with a Woolworths bit that he heated on the gas stove. This baseboard was fronted by an ebonite panel bearing the tuning dial and one or two other controls, but devoid of any sides, back or top, so that all the 'works' – including the valves which glowed faintly when the switch was on – were open to view except when their nakedness was concealed by a cloth.

Of course there were a few other bits and pieces tucked underneath, such as an accumulator and a black box housing the 'convertor' that changed the DC supply to AC. Hung on the wall was the most important item of all, the loudspeaker, now no longer trumpet-shaped but neatly contained in a polished wooden box with a fretwork design of a setting sun – or was it a rising one? – on its front.

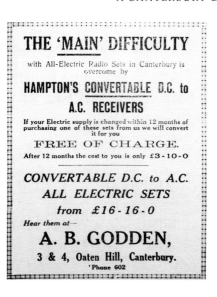

THE 'MAIN' DIFFICULTY

with All-Electric Radio Sets in Canterbury is overcome by

HAMPTON'S CONVERTABLE D.C. to A.C. RECEIVERS

If your Electric supply is changed within 12 months of purchasing one of these sets from us we will convert it for you

FREE OF CHARGE.

After 12 months the cost to you is only £3-10-0

CONVERTABLE D.C. to A.C.

ALL ELECTRIC SETS

from £16-16-0

Hear them at—

A. B. GODDEN,

3 & 4, Oaten Hill, Canterbury.

'Phone 602

In the 1920s Canterbury's electricity supply was direct current (DC) only, but with the expected arrival of alternating current (AC) people bought convertible radio receivers (wireless sets)

Amazingly, after a few teething troubles this contraption worked, drawing in not only the BBC's Home and Light programmes but also some foreign stations. Especially welcome was Radio Luxembourg, broadcasting an endless stream of light music with announcements and commercials in English, something available only from foreign stations at that time. Our living room resounded with 'Cloches de Corneville' and advertisers' theme songs such as 'We are the Ovaltineys', but undoubtedly the key broadcast was the BBC's *Nine O'Clock News*. Even my father was converted by that to the idea of listening to the wireless, and 'switching on the News' became a family ritual.

For a year or two Ron's home-made set served us well, and then my mother took the hitherto unimaginable step: she bought from Mr Rollason a splendid Philips 'all mains' set which incorporated a set of push-buttons that instantly tuned in to a range of stations. Clad in a case of fine-grained wood with a glassy lacquered finish, this served my parents throughout the war and long after.

My father had kept the wireless waiting on the doorstep when it had already entered the homes of most of my contemporaries. It did not take us long to discover, though, what a vital component of life it could be. Now it was possible not only to know how George Bernard Shaw felt about some of the problems of the contemporary world, but actually to hear him speak his thoughts in person. There was then no way of recording what we heard, so there was a ready market for a BBC publication called *The Listener* which printed the text of a good many of the talks. Of all the weeklies, this one, with its splendid pictorial supplements printed in photogravure, exactly fitted the needs of a teenager of that time. Thanks to the BBC, I was able to listen to music of sorts that I had never before encountered, such as Dvorak and Brahms, and would have known nothing of had it not come through the loudspeaker.

It was through words rather than music, however, that the BBC most profoundly influenced our lives at that time, reaching out to unformed intellects such as my own but equally to other minds, such as my parents', long contained within a carapace of customary belief. This happened through the talks and the News, but perhaps nowhere more clearly than in the programme called *Any Questions?* – but known most widely as 'The Brains Trust'. Before the coming of the wireless, few had any opportunity to eavesdrop

Ken's education was hugely broadened by family-listening to radio programmes from the BBC and, via short-wave broadcasts, from around the world

TO WIRELESS LISTENERS.

On SUNDAY, AUGUST 5th,
3.30 —— 5.0 p.m.
(British Summer Time).

Judge Rutherford

President, International Bible Students' Assn.,
will give an ADDRESS from
Detroit Coliseum, U.S.A.

Short Wave Transmitter (2XAD),
General Electric Co., Schenectady,
U.S.A., on 21.96 metres; power
50,000 Watts.

A SELECT MUSICAL PROGRAMME will
PRECEDE AND FOLLOW ADDRESS.

on the conversation of educated people and so discover how discussion could be carried on within a group. *Any Questions* brought together four or five people, most of whom would have been classed as 'intellectuals', to give their answers to questions put forward by listeners. The best-known was the philosopher C. E. M. Joad, with his famous phrase 'It all depends what you mean by …', but the biologist Julian Huxley ran him a close second, together with a breezy former naval commander, A. B. Campbell, who brought knowledge and common sense rather than intellect to the discussions.

And discussions they were, for although the original intention was perhaps to provide answers to difficult questions, it soon became apparent that the journey mattered more than the destination – that the debates were more important than the answers. Intellectuals, particularly those who had not been invited to join the Brains Trust 'panel', might – and often did – treat this programme with lofty disdain. But I have a picture in my mind – not a fanciful one – of our family of four sitting intent after a meal, listening to the Brains Trust and learning in the process that debate is much more than assertion and rebuttal; that in a small group ideas can be tossed from mind to mind, played with and made more visible by exposure. Whatever we had heard in sermons or speeches, or read in print, were monologues; here was an ensemble, and one whose concert we could all enjoy.

Such enjoyment, and the enlargement of life that went with it, is rarely possible today, for civilized discussion on the radio has become a rarity. There is no waiting nowadays for the moment when an interjection can be slipped in without wrecking the speaker's train of thought. The interviewers now in command cannot have been taught in infancy that it is rude to interrupt – they do it all the time, often so outrageously that at last some of the unfortunate victims have begun to strike back with phrases such as 'Let me finish.'

Like every other aspect of life at that time, the BBC bore the clear imprint of the middle classes. As newcomers to the new national pastime of 'listening in', we soon came to the conclusion that British broadcasting was ruled by a benevolent despot named Sir John Reith, and that it was largely thanks to him that we could expect to hear no swearing or smutty jokes coming through our loudspeaker. It went almost without saying that all the announcers would speak the King's English in a 'cultivated accent', and we were not surprised to learn (I think from the *Radio Times*) that they were required to don evening dress before reading the radio News at nine o'clock!

At an early stage in its history, the BBC earned a nickname – 'Auntie' – that has stuck ever since. My parents approved of 'Auntie's' stance, and although she seemed to be a very strait-laced old dame, Ron and I were prepared to tolerate her. Then in 1936 we were all stricken with doubt. That was the year in which King George V died. Instantly, all levity vanished from radio programmes. There was no light music, and even classical music with any hint of joyfulness was banned. We were by no means anti-monarchist, and my parents never wavered in their belief in the need to keep the stream of radio running pure and clear. But suddenly it struck us, as never before, that if not in Heaven then in Portland Place, there was someone who believed he knew how it was proper for us to think, feel and act at that moment in the nation's history. For all his sympathy with Reith's outlook, my father became incensed by the BBC's overbearing gloom.

Two or three years later, one icy morning in March, I sat with about two hundred others in the great hall of Christ Church, Oxford, waiting to find out the subject of the essay that I and all the others were to write as part of a scholarship examination. On each side of the hall, huge log fires blazed with a fierceness that would roast those nearby and create a small temperate zone between them and the frozen fringe. I found a seat that avoided both extremes, and as I sat down my thoughts flew for a moment to what I knew must be just below my feet – the college kitchen, in which my father had worked as a boy half a century earlier. But only for a moment, for there was the single sheet in front of me with the essay subject: 'Words'.

Since my mother's purchase of the Philips radio, I had listened to the whole world, even America on the short wave band. Words, words, endless words – and what did they all amount to? All around me I could see bewildered candidates scratching their heads and knitting their brows. But my listening to the wireless left me in no doubt as to what to write about – the propaganda wars that were raging between rival 'isms', and the way in which psychology and technology had been yoked together in support of this worldwide battle. My starting point was the biblical quotation (a typically Reithian touch) that appeared for a time on the masthead of the *Radio Times*: 'Nation shall speak peace unto nation.' I had little difficulty in demonstrating how utterly this pious hope was contradicted by what was actually happening; and from that, I went on to examine the techniques that were being used in this war of words.

Wireless had already woven itself into our lives, delivering information and sparking ideas in a way that was far more effective than the *New Popular Educator* that Ron and I had persuaded our parents to buy in weekly parts in our early teens. So there I was in the hall of Christ Church, scribbling away as lunchtime smells began to rise from its nether regions, inspired not so much by books I had read as by sounds I had heard thanks to this novelty, wireless or radio, which had so lately and grudgingly been admitted to our home.

With the coming of war, 'the wireless' became even more an integral part of my family's and the nation's life. Through our loudspeakers we heard Churchill's tribute to 'the few' who had fought and won the Battle of Britain, and his grim picture in 1940 of the way ahead as one of 'blood, toil, sweat and tears'. But there was another voice that many listened to, some with misgivings as to whether or not they were doing something unpatriotic, others with curiosity and suspended belief. This was 'Lord Haw-Haw' as he was nicknamed, an Irishman named William Joyce who was the main German propagandist broadcasting to British listeners. Speaking from Hamburg in harsh, rather nasal tones, he asked insistently in the early years of the war, 'Where is the *Ark Royal?*', knowing that the sinking of this great warship, with a terrible loss of life, had been concealed from the British public by Churchill because he feared it would have a devastating effect on public morale.

Joyce went on broadcasting his mixture of information and misinformation until the end of the war, when he was captured, tried and executed as a traitor, even though he had never been a British citizen. My old school friend from Whitstable, Victor West, wrote a poem – perhaps the last he ever penned – about Joyce entitled 'Germany Calling Germany'. Vic maintained that Joyce lived in Whitstable for a time before the war, sometimes making speeches at Starvation Point in support of the British Union of Fascists. The poem, 'Germany Calling Germany', was not one of Vic's best, but he could be forgiven for that, for by the time he wrote it he was at death's door, gasping for breath even when inhaling oxygen in order to sustain a conversation on the telephone. But as to the fact that Joyce had really been his neighbour, Vic was in no doubt at all.

Taken captive in Crete (where he had found that just a year of Greek at the Langton had provided him with the means to communicate with the locals), Vic was shipped to Greece and then to a prisoner of war camp in Germany. Here, wireless became crucial to him, for a set was smuggled into the camp hidden in an accordion that was sent to a prisoner through the Red Cross. This gave him and others some idea of how the war was going, and it provided Vic with material for the 'pep talks' that he delivered from time to time. After the war, Vic did a painting that recalled the scene as a group of prisoners listened to one of Churchill's broadcasts. He offered the picture to Churchill, and for a time it hung on the walls of Chartwell. After Churchill's death, it was lost, but fortunately a preliminary sketch survives – to me, a reminder of two great figures: one known to the world and to history, the other to a privileged handful of whom I am one.

One strand of the story of my childhood is how the wireless entered our household as an uninvited guest and then became part of the family in peace and war. This was a revolutionary change, yet now I see it as just the first stage of something far greater – the harnessing of the power of the electron to serve every sort of human need. 'Electronics' was a word I never heard in my school-days, yet today it figures in every aspect of our daily lives from cars to computers. That was something I never dreamed of as, trembling, I crept with Kenneth Miles into the basement room of his house in Dane John over eighty years ago.

7

Sin and Cinema

A FRENZY OF building was going on in Canterbury seventy-five years ago. Two great new cinemas were being built, one called the Regal, in St George's Place, and the other at the opposite end of the main street, provisionally called 'The Picture House', but eventually named 'The Friars' after its location. My bricklayer friend, Stan Ellis, told me that sometimes there were 400 men on the Regal site, working all the hours of daylight and even on Sundays. That

In 1933 The Friars won the race to become Canterbury's first 'super-cinema'

posed a problem for Stan, as he was one of our Sunday School teachers. There was the same picture of frantic activity at the other end of the main street, for the two cinemas were racing to be the first to open, spurred by the thought that the winner would be opened by our MP, Sir William Wayland, while the loser would have to be content with the Mayor. From the first announcements to the opening ceremonies, only sixteen weeks elapsed, with The Friars winning by a short head.

At the Regal site the hoardings were stripped away as soon as the entrance had been completed, and as I walked to school from our new house in New Dover Road I eagerly scanned the Art Deco panels on its pillars in which stills of some of the forthcoming films were slotted. As the building neared completion, my parents received an invitation to the opening ceremony, together with an elaborate brochure, of which every page was interleaved with translucent paper bearing a spider's web design, describing the architectural merits, the auditorium, the ballroom and café, and all the other glories of the Regal, in enticing detail.

Two days after the grand opening, I was able to go and see this wonder for myself. The air of luxury was staggering. There were acres of wall-to-wall carpet, at a time when most people had to be content with chilly linoleum or even Darkalined bare boards; it was deliciously warm, banishing thoughts of the unheated bedrooms, bed socks and hot water bottles that awaited nearly all of its customers. There were wall lights that came only timidly to life; usherettes in smart uniforms that harmonized with the rest of the décor; and even a delicate, if synthetic, odour of spring flowers – perhaps a necessary refinement, for I had already become aware from Sunday School of what some people unkindly called 'the great unwashed'. The walls of the auditorium were gilded from floor to ceiling, and embossed with cunning plasterwork, a fit setting for the greatest marvel of all, the Compton organ that rose to view, already in full blast, blushing with a myriad colours. The famous organist Reginald Foort put the organ through its paces, showing how it could simulate drums, xylophone, castanets, surf,

At the Regal cinema (now the Odeon) audiences were entertained by the marvels of the Compton Organ, rising majestically from the floor in glorious changing colours. The Regal also boasted a restaurant and a ballroom

railways, a whistle and an aeroplane; and finally layer on layer of gauzy curtains parted to show on stage a piano that played, as if by an invisible hand, the tune that he fingered on the console. It was all a far cry from Mr W. T. Harvey ARCO and his tiny band of fiddlers in the pit of the St George's Picture Theatre a couple of hundred yards away.

These two 'super-cinemas', as everyone was now calling them, seated about 3,000 people, the greatest secular audience the city had seen since Roman times, and perhaps the greatest ever. They represented an explosion of popular entertainment that hardly any of the inhabitants would have thought possible a few years earlier. Yet once they were open, there was no shortage of customers, for long queues formed every night. It was a revolution in the social life of this city. Why did it happen just then, in August 1933, and why was it on such a huge scale? As I sat in the comfort of the Regal, watching Bombardier Billy Wells wield a huge hammer to

115

hit a colossal gong, announcing a new British film, or saw the Metro-Goldwyn-Mayer lion sleepily roaring to welcome something good from Hollywood, I did not ask any such questions. But I cannot resist asking them now.

Cinema, or 'the pictures' as we almost always called it, was nothing new to Canterbury. The Electric Theatre had opened in 1911, the St George's in 1915, and the Central – replacing the Electric – in 1928. Even earlier, films had sometimes been shown in fairgrounds or theatres: on the wall of Debenhams' department store in Guildhall Street there is a plaque commemorating the first showing of a film in the city in 1896 at the former Theatre Royal. At first I went with Ron to the St George's or the Central, but from the age of nine or ten I was allowed to go alone, always to afternoon performances, so we never had to queue. If anyone had asked us in 1930 or even 1932 (which of course they never did) whether we thought Canterbury needed 3,000 more cinema seats, we would have answered 'Nonsense'. And most of our elders would have agreed.

Yet, if only I had been able to recognize it, I had warning that this great change was coming. Sitting in the Central one Saturday afternoon in 1930, I waited for the lights to go down so that I could move back into the dearer seats. The man next to me told me of the palatial cinemas he had seen in America. I was deeply impressed, but thought little more about it. After all, such wonders could never come to our part of the world. I did not know that the idea of super-cinemas had already crossed the Atlantic and landed at Dover, where the Granada was to open later in the year.

Its name had been given, said the *Kentish Gazette*, 'out of compliment to that sunny spot in Spain, with its gorgeous Moorish architecture, reminiscences of which have been successfully recalled by the architect'. It was an instant success, drawing not only local people, but others from far afield. From Canterbury each weekend, coach parties of about a hundred converged on the Granada. At nine shillings and sixpence for the fare and entry ticket combined – about a fifth of many a working man's weekly wage – it was far more than a visit to one of the local cinemas would have cost. But it was a 'night out', in good company. A rather cheaper alternative was the great new cinema only seven miles away at Tankerton, called the Troc, which could be reached by the ordinary and frequent bus route. The local papers gave long previews, all written in a rapturous style which might be called Wardour Street English, not only to the two city cinemas but those on the coast as well.

Clearly there was money to be made from this growing passion for films, especially if they were shown in a new sort of cinema. In Canterbury the Regal project got under way, piloted by a group of Canterbury businessmen under the chairman of the Invicta motor company, Mr J. B. Thompson, and The Friars site was acquired by the nationwide Odeon chain whose chairman was Oscar Deutsch. In contrast to other cinemas in the chain, they found themselves unable to use the name 'Odeon' because it had already been claimed by the former Electric Cinema, which had become the Odeon Hall.

Oblivious to what was hatching, I concentrated on quite another aspect of film-going in Canterbury – the arrival of the 'talkies', which came to the Central. In 1930, two years after it had opened, I had been quite happy to watch silent films, with Mr Harvey's band stirring the blood with *prestissimo* tunes to accompany the exploits of Rin-Tin-Tin, the dog with an almost human intelligence, or playing 'Felix goes on walking', of which I knew both the tune and the words, as I watched the cartoon antics of Felix the Cat, a predecessor of Mickey Mouse. On one occasion, too, there was a film in which words and music appeared on the screen and a lady in evening dress came on stage to warble and give us the opportunity to join in. As we filed out I had a furious argument with Ron. I was sure that the singer was one of the usherettes, who had dumped the torch with which she guided people to their sets, changed her dress, and then performed. Ron contemptuously dismissed this idea, and I felt deeply hurt.

Very soon, however, I was able to see for myself the added impact the talkies could give to films. Some school friends told me that if I went to the Central at the end of the afternoon, about the time when the performance ended, I would see something interesting. The film was *The Singing Fool*, starring Al Jolson. It was a real tear-jerker, a genre with a long history of success in Canterbury, for Councillor Stone once remarked that anyone going to *East Lynne* at the Theatre Royal, which ended with the death of a noblewoman's illegitimate child, needed to take an umbrella if they sat under the edge of the balcony. Full of songs delivered by Jolson as a black-face comedian, a story quite outside the scope of any silent film, it ended with the required death scene. With the callousness of youth, I watched with glee as the audience, mostly of women and many of them sobbing convulsively, filed out into St Margaret's Street.

Not surprisingly, the local press pronounced the Central's switch to the 'eagerly awaited "talkies"' a great success. Yet strangely, the St George's did not follow suit. Anyone who was interested – and that did not include me – was able to learn why when, in August 1930, the *Kentish Gazette* printed, for the first and the last time ever, an account of the annual general meeting of the company. It ran to two or three columns, most of it being devoted to an impassioned speech by the manager, Mr J. H. Wills. He had some difficult explaining to do. To begin with, the dividend, which had been 15 per cent for years, had been cut to 5 per cent because of the competition from the Central. Mr Wills felt sure, however, that the shareholders would agree with him and his directors that the decision not to 'go talkie' had been the right one. The cost of wiring the theatre for sound would have run them into deficit, and the dividend would have been nil. Moreover, the talkies were a flash in the pan, a will-o'-the-wisp that they would have been foolish to pursue. He staked this view on a lifetime spent in the entertainment business, during which he had appeared before the footlights of all the main theatres in the country. Whatever criticisms had been levelled at him were 'not cricket'. In Canterbury at that time, that was pretty well the strongest expression anyone could use without lapsing into vulgar abuse.

I knew nothing of all this, but what I was aware of was that towards the end of the year the St George's 'went talkie' with a minimum of publicity and a modest increase in admission prices. It staggered on until 1934, closing because of what was acknowledged to be the overwhelming competition from the new super-cinemas. As I read the *Gazette*'s obituary article, I felt an intense pang of nostalgia at its mention of the local operatic society's production of *The Gondoliers*. That evening was one of the two evenings of my young life that were touched with glory. The other was the performance of *Cinderella* that I was taken to in the last days of the Theatre Royal, when to my amazement a coach came on stage drawn by a real horse – well, a real *pony* anyway. But re-reading that piece many years – indeed, many decades – later, I am struck by something else: that while there is understandably no mention of the unfortunate Mr Wills, there is also hardly anything about the showing of films, to which this 'picture theatre' was devoted almost exclusively throughout the nineteen years of its existence. Instead the writer recalls what he sees as the notable events in the theatre's history, the performances of the operatic society and especially of the Old Stagers, which had caused noblemen such as the Earl of Dartmouth and Lord Harris to join the audience.

Clearly the writer saw this cinema as a place of artless entertainment, patronized mainly by the poor, about which there was nothing much to say. What he wrote – and still more, what he did not write – is an indication of what a low opinion of cinema there was among the more articulate section of the population, many of whom looked back with nostalgia and forward with hope to real, not celluloid, theatre. The local press was full of laments at the lack of a really adequate theatre. The Canterbury Dramatic Society had to use the Foresters' and the County halls, each with only minimal backstage facilities, or to hire the Odeon Hall for a week, for productions that often won national awards. When the

St George's closed, a prescient correspondent to the local papers suggested its conversion to a theatre named after Marlowe. Some negotiations then took place, but they came to nothing, and in due course the building was converted into a Co-operative store.

The yearning for live theatre was renewed year by year at the Canterbury Festival, at which new plays of great merit by writers such as Christopher Fry, Dorothy L. Sayers and, above all, T. S. Eliot, were presented. A school friend of mine left a vivid impression on me by his account of a rehearsal of *Murder in the Cathedral*: the townsfolk of Canterbury, my friend among them, chanting Eliot's verse in the gloom of the Chapter House, and then a tall figure entering from the Cloisters to stand at the back, listening intently.

What few of the campaigners for live theatre remembered was how troubled the end of the old Theatre Royal had been. Given to the city by the famous artist Sidney Cooper in the 1860s, it had been inherited by his son Nigel, who visited the Beaney every week to hand over a sheaf of free tickets in order to ensure that the theatre should not look too depressingly empty. Eventually, Pickfords, the carriers, had a standing rule that no scenery was to be delivered except on prepayment, and it was well known that on Fridays a queue of landladies would form at the stage door to ensure they got their rents before the actors had the chance to liquidate their wages. By the time he gave up the struggle, Nigel Cooper had lost £10,000.

The famous actress Dame Sybil Thorndike, whom I was later to see on screen wielding a warming pan for one of Charles Laughton's bridal beds in *The Private Life of Henry VIII*, gave a powerful push to the live theatre campaign by delivering a lecture at the Festival in 1934 on 'The Responsibilities of the Theatre to the Community'. It made a deep impression, and led directly to the opening – which she would have performed herself if she had been free – of a repertory theatre in the Odeon later that year, replacing the dances and something called 'Krazy Nights' that had taken place there since the closure of the Electric Theatre.

Under two managements, with a period in between of 'Old Time Music Hall', the 'Rep', as everyone called it, lasted until the outbreak of war closed all places of entertainment for a while. The life that its little bands of actors led must have been very like the one depicted by J. B. Priestley in *The Good Companions*: small audiences, short commons, intense dedication to their art. On at least one occasion they abandoned a production halfway through the week, substituting another that they thought might have more box office appeal. It was a relief when the Old Time Music Hall phase ended, for although I and my schoolfellows in the balcony dutifully roared out the choruses, our hearts – or at least mine – were not in it. Then the plays resumed, some of them new West End productions that embodied ideas that were strong meat for a Canterbury audience. One of my acquaintances, Tony Gibbs, who had gone on from Miss Pierce's to the cathedral choir school, found himself next to one of the canons in the 'gents' during the interval at the Rep, to hear the muttered advice, 'Mum's the word.'

Unlike the cinemas, the Rep never reopened after the emergency closures in 1939, and at last The Friars was able to adopt the name of Odeon which it had long coveted – a name that, confusingly, now adorns what I knew as the Regal. In its short and chequered career, the Rep had shown that the end of the Theatre Royal was no accident; for despite all the campaigners' plaints, theatre-goers were too thin on the ground to sustain a theatre adequately. Yet that is not the whole story: a tradition had been established that must have paved the way for the civic theatre, the Marlowe, which took over the Central's building soon after the war ended.

The cinema had won – that is to say, it had won the battle of numbers and box-office takings. The battle of esteem, the attempt to overcome the air of disrepute that surrounded cinemas, was quite another matter. A few years before my birth the Lancashire education authority asked a number of its teachers what they thought of this new medium of mass entertainment. With the exception of one sturdy individualist, all those consulted agreed that 'cinematograph shows were physically detrimental to the scholars in consequence of the late hours, loss of sleep and the bad atmosphere'. Worse still was the mental effect on the children, making them 'fond of noise, ostentatious display, self-advertisement and change. The pictures excited their minds and created a love of pleasure and a disinclination for work and effort.'

Had my parents known of this damning indictment, they might have forbidden my visits to the cinema, but they must have been aware that local religious leaders took an equally dim view of film-going. In a Council debate in 1930, Frank Hooker, a pillar of the Baptist Church, said that it was 'very serious to see people queuing up to go to cinemas, and spending money which they had not earned; or, if they had earned it, spending money which they ought to save'.

He spoke in the authentic tones of Puritanism, echoing sentiments of 300 years before, castigating in one breath the pursuit of pleasure and the waste of money on fripperies. It was not long before the established Church chipped in. The Vicar of Thanington, the Revd V. T. Macy, described in a letter to the *Kentish Gazette* how, caught by a sudden storm, he had taken refuge in a cinema where he saw a film starring Pola Negri. It contained 'a disgusting scene of sexual passion' and ended with the heroine, Pola Negri of course, being tried for the murder of her lover. She was acquitted: the verdict was false and the audience knew it, but to Mr Macy's dismay they broke into spontaneous applause.

I sensed that an atmosphere of disapproval, even perhaps a whiff of sin, seemed to surround cinemas. Yet I don't remember anyone suggesting that my visits to 'the pictures' might lead me into moral danger. I knew from Harold Copping's illustrations to Bunyan's *Pilgrim's Progress*, which my grandfather had presented to my mother on her eleventh birthday, that life's journey was not without its perils – a lesson that was vividly reinforced by a pictorial representation of Bunyan's tale that hung in my grandparents' back bedroom. It showed Christian's straight and narrow path stretching upwards from the bottom frame, and close to the top there was a slip road which, if one ignored the 'No Entry' signs, would land the traveller slap in the centre of Vanity Fair.

I was thus aware of that peril, and of course my mother was even more so. But she reserved her lecture on that topic for my teens. Naming no names, and speaking only in general terms, she warned me of the possibility of getting entangled with 'worldly' people. I knew well what she was getting at: for reasons that had nothing whatever to do with religious zeal, I had persuaded a young friend to induce his sweet and shapely elder sister to join our Sunday School and become my first and short-lived girl-friend. But no special measures were needed to limit my cinema-going, and so avoid the danger of addiction. Economics performed that function, for my pocket money of threepence allowed only occasional visits at fourpence-halfpenny. In family discussions, films might be disparaged as 'silly', especially Laurel and Hardy, but not, for some unexplained reason, Charlie Chaplin, but that was all.

So, thanks to my parents' tolerance, for which I remain surprised and grateful, going to the pictures was a permitted if occasional pleasure. I must have started at the age of eight or nine, for I went once to the Electric Theatre before it closed in 1928. I have no recollection of the film, but the red sign over the exit into Black Griffin Lane imprinted itself on my memory, to be recalled years later when I saw a cartoon in *Punch* that showed a bearded old man pointing to the 'Exit' sign – one such as I recalled – and asking the usherette, 'How do you justify that third person singular?'

Likewise, my parents had no serious misgivings to swallow when they attended the opening of the Regal. Not so, I imagine, their fellow nonconformist, Frank Hooker. Only three years previously he had described cinema-going as a serious problem, yet now, as Mayor, it was his duty to welcome one of the two greatest cinemas the city had ever seen. His resolution of this dilemma might have come straight from *Roget's Thesaurus*. In place of the gangster and cowboy type of film, he said, he hoped this new theatre would grasp the opportunity to show films that were clean, wholesome, uplifting, helpful, stimulating and educative, so that when people went they would be uplifted as well as amused.

A new medium of entertainment so powerful and pervasive as film was bound to come into collision sooner or later with established practices and ideas. In Canterbury, as in almost everywhere else of any significance in the country, cinemas excited debates throughout the 1930s. Sometimes these concerned the content and social effects of films; clearly, Mr Macy feared that people were beginning to get their ideas of morality from the screen rather than the pulpit. But the main emphasis was on something quite otherwise – the question of when films should be shown.

In an age when few feel summoned by bells on the seventh day of the week, and for most people the main duty of that morning is washing the car, it is difficult to imagine the depth of emotion that surrounded the question of 'the shape of Sunday' two or three generations ago. A glance through the local papers of 1930 shows the importance it then assumed. At Deal, there is a meeting of protest so crowded that its proceedings are relayed to hundreds of people who can't get into the hall. A message of support from the Archbishop of Canterbury is read out to the audience. What they are protesting about is a proposal before the local Council to open the municipal tennis courts for play on Sundays. In Whitstable, a well-known entrepreneur, Mr Arthur Fitt, is proposing to build a huge new cinema called the Troc at Tankerton. The application goes to appeal, and Mr Mowll, a solicitor representing a number of religious bodies, objects on the grounds that there are already enough cinemas in Whitstable, and above all that Mr Fitt has said that it would be essential for the Troc to open on Sundays – otherwise it would be uneconomic. Mr Mowll quotes a quatrain by a former Lord Chief Justice which he has seen displayed on railway stations:

A Sabbath well spent brings a week of content
And health for the toils of tomorrow.
But a Sabbath profaned, whatever else may be gained
Is a certain forerunner of sorrow.

But despite this poetic opposition, Mr Fitt wins, and the Troc rises and, for a time, flourishes before being demolished and the site given over to hard tennis courts.

In Canterbury, far less influenced than its seaside neighbours by the need to provide 'visitor attractions' that would benefit the local economy, the debate about Sunday took a different turn. It was sparked off by an application for a licence for the Central Cinema to hold a Sunday evening concert at 8.15 p.m., well after church hours. Alderman Barrett, always in favour of what he saw as 'progress' and not in sympathy with the influential nonconformist group of councillors, described how the cinema had recently installed 'apparatus to provide the very best music by mechanical means'. Therefore permission was asked 'to show on the screen the artists who were playing in that mechanical orchestra' – nothing more. He added that he was not in favour of films being shown in any of the city's cinemas on Sundays. In the ensuing discussion he made it clear that no 'live' artist would be involved, and even the projectionists would give their services free.

Barrett got his way – or, his opponents later felt, he got away with it; for it was not long before they saw through his talk of 'mechanical' orchestras and artists, and of the film that was not a film yet needed the help of projectionists. In later years Hooker and Lefevre, both Baptist stalwarts who became Mayor, united in describing this moment as 'the thin edge of the wedge'.

Perhaps it was, but the defenders of 'the old English Sunday', a phrase that completely overlooked the fierce debates about Sunday and the Sabbath of the seventeenth century, were fighting a hopeless battle against popular demand. I had little interest in charity concerts, whether on Sundays or weekdays. But in 1935,

the Sunday question came home to me. By then the charity concerts had become established and were gaining even greater
popularity by introducing a new type of performer, comedians
and singers made famous by radio. 'A galaxy of wireless stars'
was a phrase often used in the advertisements. Capacity audiences came to see the comedian Stainless Stephen, who raised
laughs by enunciating all the punctuation marks of his patter, or
the child impersonator Harry Hemsley, and many another whose
names evoke no echo today.

The bandmaster of the Canterbury City Band, Mr Beckwith,
saw possibilities not to be missed. In 1935 he applied for a licence
to perform a Sunday concert. It was to be for charity, of course,
with half the proceeds going to the band's funds and half to the
new hospital appeal. The band would play Schubert's music
while the film *Blossom Time* was being shown. As it had done
before, the Council divided along lines already scored by 300
years of history. The Mayor, Charles Lefevre (later to be Mayor
again in the darkest days of the war), said he thought it was time
to 'state we are going to keep Sunday a little bit as it was in the old
days'. Speaking both as Sheriff and as a churchwarden, Councillor Surtees dissented: 'I would ask opponents to visualize the
position of some of those living in the poorer parts of Canterbury.
Many of them are living in a small room with the only alternative
of walking the streets. I should like to see some form of entertainment in Canterbury between 8 and 10 p.m. throughout the
winter.' Finally, Councillor Sheppard, the pastor of the Roman
Catholic church of St Thomas, reminded the councillors that 8
p.m. was after church hours. 'It is very true indeed that the young
men and women have nothing to do on Sunday nights. The
Sabbath was made for man, not man for the Sabbath.'

The motion was passed by fifteen votes to seven. This immediately posed a problem for my father. For years he had been a
great supporter of the City Band, which I had known first as the
Silver Band and then under its later name. My father took me to
band contests in Tunbridge Wells, and then to even greater ones

in the Crystal Palace before that wonderful creation was burnt down in 1933, being replaced for subsequent band contests by the faded grandeur of the Alexandra Palace. When my father died in 1950, he left a mass of band accounts that I wish I had preserved. Although he never returned to playing the euphonium, the chosen instrument of his youth, the band was one of the main pre-occupations of his leisure time.

With the granting of Mr Beckwith's licence, my father's long-standing connection with the band ended abruptly. His opposition to Sunday performances was a matter of principle, and on that there could be no compromise. A few years later, a similar crisis arose when his church, the Congregational in Watling Street, proposed to admit a single mother (a term yet to be invented) to full membership. After more than twenty years as office holder and Sunday School superintendent, he left, and with my mother migrated to the Baptist church.

From the bare facts of these two turning points in my parents' lives, they may seem a dour and blue-nosed pair. In fact, they were nothing like that. On our family holiday in Oxford, my father got us some of the best seats in the New Theatre to see the comedian George Robey, a famous figure whose bushy eyebrows had graced every hoarding in Oxford for weeks beforehand with the simple message 'He's coming'. Beyond telling me, in answer to some of my questions, that celebrities such as the great comedian often had very unhappy private lives (a generalization that surely few would quarrel with), he had nothing adverse to say about the stage and its professionals. He loved fireworks and gave us splendid backyard performances each Guy Fawkes night, at a cost that made my mother blench. But he could not accept the intrusion of public performances, whether live, projected, or a combination of both, into the sacred tranquillity of Sunday.

Today, the language of the opponents of Sunday entertainment seems quaint and their conclusions often overstated or plain wrong. But this should not blind us to the fact that they had grasped something real – that cinemas were a social force of undeniable importance, especially after the explosion of audience numbers. I might be tempted to try to analyse how films cracked the crust of custom, softening up their audiences for the coming of the consumer society as they saw manifestations of the American way of life such as the vast fridges in the background of Laurel and Hardy comedies. I might point out how, when Mr Smith went to Washington, we learned that shirts could have an attached collar instead of one that had to be affixed with a back and a front stud. I might speculate that Hollywood made us America's neighbours, creating a 'special relationship' long before diplomats discovered that idea, and argue that Bernard Shaw's remark about 'two nations divided by a common language' was clever but wrong.

But I refuse to do any of these things. Instead I will stick to my last, which is Canterbury and my own experiences as a child growing up there. Just how the power of the cinema to mould society exerted itself may be open to debate, but that it existed is surely undeniable. In Canterbury alone, the power of films to draw unprecedented audiences, to make them laugh and cry, is evidence enough. The bland assurance of Lefevre and Hooker in 1930 that their own views on the observance of Sunday could be imposed indefinitely on the people at large was soon revealed as the thinking of a bygone age. These two and their like-minded friends on the Council were good men who did great things for their city; for a while, the population might be willing to follow their lead on account of the good governance they had provided. But only for a while: in the heat of politics, gratitude quickly evaporates, and soon there were many who could see no sufficient reason why they should not have on Sundays pretty much the enjoyments available on weekdays. The 'love of pleasure' foreseen by the Lancashire teachers twenty years earlier had become widespread, even if it was not attended by the tribe of troubles that they also foresaw.

Where, then, did this power come from? What was its secret? The answer is, I think, very simple: that these were pictures that *moved* – motion pictures, or 'movies', to use the American terms. Photographs were all very well, but photographs that moved were something phenomenal. That was why at first it was enough simply to show films to draw in spectators at fairgrounds.

So also at home. One Christmas Ron had a new toy, a German-made tinplate projector lit by an oil lamp and so sporting a chimney. Each of its films lasted barely a minute. They were simply offcuts, full size and appallingly flammable (though the word we would have used was 'inflammable'), sweepings from the floor of some film studio. To the loud clanking of the sprocket wheels, they ran through the projector in a flash, far too short a time to tell any sort of story. But they moved. We saw a lady lower a fan and reveal her face. And that was it: the film fell on the floor and Ron threaded another piece in.

The advent of the talkies and the imaginative marketing that inspired the super-cinemas each gave a tremendous boost to film-going. Even so, movement was, and remains, the basic attraction of film. Early in the history of the art, the Americans started calling films 'motion pictures' or 'movies', terms that have stuck while 'talkies' has become defunct. Thanks to DVDs it is now easy – more so than ever before – to look back to the early days of cinemas. We are able not only to ask, but also perhaps to answer, the question: what induced some Canterbury citizen to gut a medieval building in 1911 and convert it into a cinema? What induced the shareholders of the St George's four years later to put their money into setting up a new, purpose-built cinema, St George's Gate? What kind of film shows did these two put on, and how did they compare with what was on offer at the Theatre Royal?

The answer is astonishing. When films of the pre-1914 era are shown to a modern audience from a DVD, the result is gales of laughter. Some examples of a series of films based on the works of Dickens survive, for instance. The flimsy scenery, the wildly exaggerated gestures and expressions of the actors, the confusing plots, and the banal titles (such as 'A Happy Ending', followed by a blob of a full stop) all excite hilarity. There is one in this series made by the great American director, D. W. Griffith, whose *Birth of a Nation* is recognized as a landmark in the history of film. It is a little less awful than the others, but only a little. It was not very long, of course, before movie makers, especially in America, realized that movement was the great advantage they had to exploit, and that film gave them a wide variety of completely novel storytelling opportunities, such as 'intercutting' from one scene to another and back again. By the early 1920s, they had built up a great fund of expertise in using film to tell a story. But when the two cinemas started up in Canterbury, directors had advanced only a little way along that path. The fact that films were pictures that moved was enough – it had to be – for most of their patrons.

By the time I started going to the 'pictures', the absurdities of the early days had long been outgrown. One day I saw two great posters outside the Electric Theatre advertising a film called *Ben Hur*. I had read about the great chariot race, and I pictured it in my mind's eye. I took in the fact that thousands of actors had been involved, and that the production had cost nearly a million pounds. I longed to go, but somehow there was never a chance. A few years later, in Woolworths, I bought a copy of Lew Wallace's book on which the film was based, but I gave up trying to read it long before I reached the chariot race. Had I managed to get to the cinema, I am sure I would have been absorbed from the first minute of the film.

How was it that film could give its audiences this deep and almost instant sense of involvement? Intellectuals did their best to find an explanation. Jean-Luc Godard said that film was 'reality twenty-four times a second'. But by the age of ten or eleven I had come to my own conclusion, a simple one but durable enough to last a lifetime – that though the film-goer's involvement in the world on the screen, blotting out the world of the everyday, might be inexplicable, it was certainly undeniable. This realization came to me on that fateful Saturday afternoon at the Central in 1930 when I first learned of the super-cinemas from the man who had been to America. He sat on my right, but on my left there was an old lady who had nothing to say until the film started. Before I was able to move back to the better seats, the plot had advanced to a crisis. A man aimed his gun, and his opponent fell to the ground. We heard the shot, for the Central had already 'gone talkie', but it would have been just as convincing if the film had been silent. The old lady nearly jumped out of her seat. 'Cor, ain't he a good shot!' she exclaimed. I had to stifle a laugh, but then I realized that she had been living in the film – an experience that had often been mine too.

8

ℰℰℬℰ

As soon as I had learned my ABC, I seemed continually to come across the mysterious letters 'CCBC'. They were boldly inscribed in white on the dun-coloured dustcarts, and highlighted in greeny-yellow on every lamp-post. Gradually it came home to me this was not a word but initials, which formed a symbol of the authority wielded by the Corporation. And what was the Corporation? Its proper title was, I gathered, the City Council, our elected governors who sat in conclave in a building called the Guildhall at the far end of the same street in which I went to school at Miss Pierce's. Here was to be found the hidden hand that organized the battalions of sweepers and cleaners of the cattle market and the streets, which had set up the City Council elementary school off Northgate, which had established the local Electricity Works to generate power for the whole city, which had … but the list was endless. Above all, this was the body that had ringed the city with hundreds of council houses, at low rents. Just as the standards of the legions bore the letters SPQR to denote the might of Rome, so CCBC was shorthand for the authority of the local Council.

We knew, of course, that its authority was not unlimited. If one of life's great necessities, electricity, was a Corporation matter, other vital services were provided by free enterprise in the shape of the Canterbury Gas and Water Company, to whose handsome (and, of course, gas-lit) offices in Castle Street my mother might

Even in the mid-1930s most houses in Canterbury were not connected to mains electricity, and the Corporation's generating plant produced only direct current (DC)

take me to pay a bill or report a leaking tap – which would quickly be re-washered by the Company free of charge. I was vaguely aware, too, that beyond the Corporation there was yet another authority, the Kent County Council at Maidstone; and beyond that the greatest of all, the Parliament in London, which was the ruler not only of our own country but – Miss Pierce assured us – also of 'the greatest empire ever seen – an empire on which the sun never sets'. The poetry of her glowing declamation implanted in our minds a sense of dominion over palm and pine which needed no confirmation by such mundane visual aids as red-speckled maps or globes.

How our Corporation related to the confusing array of other assemblies we were not too sure, but there was a general sense that somehow the Council was by no means an insignificant player. How widespread and deep the sense of local people was that the Council really mattered, that in addition to providing essential services it could react constructively in a crisis, came home to me when I began to read the local papers at the age of eleven or twelve. The economic collapse ensuing from the great American slump of 1929 penetrated, in the next year or two, to every corner of the United Kingdom. Today this would be seen as a problem, to be dealt with almost entirely by the government of the day. But in Canterbury at that time councillors and public alike leapt to the conclusion that the sudden growth of unemployment was something that should – and could – be grappled with locally as well as nationally, even though the city's thousand unemployed were only 7 per cent of the workforce, compared with 14 per cent in Herne Bay and nearly 18 per cent in Whitstable.

Every day, as I looked across the cattle market to Upper Bridge Street, I saw the 'unemployment problem' vividly portrayed in local terms, in the shape of a long queue of men (with hardly ever a woman among them) lined up outside a rather shabby shop called the Employment Exchange. Clearly the Labour Exchange, as it was commonly called, had few if any jobs to offer, and most of the callers came out after a brief interview clutching the 'dole'. This meagre sum presented them with a choice between self-indulgence and duty, for they could either keep nine pence of it in their pockets until 3 p.m., when it would buy three hours of warmth and entertainment at the St George's Picture Theatre nearby, or use that same sum at Mr Lemar's open-fronted fruit and vegetable shop in Dover Street to buy a week's supply of potatoes for their family.

Immediately opposite the Labour Exchange a beautifully designed hoarding (or billboard as it is now called in Anglo-American) had lately been erected on the railings of the cattle market, in which posters by Abram Games and other artists of the first rank presented the idea of 'Empire Free Trade' – of keeping international trade within the Empire, to the exclusion of other countries – as one solution to the re-ordering of the world economy. This government propaganda provided me with the first art gallery I had ever come across, but the policy it advocated was futile. The Council's own reactions were far more down-to-earth. It set up an Unemployment Committee to consider ways and means of creating new jobs. Following its recommendations, the Council decided to commit more than £2,000 of its income from the rates (the local property tax which was equivalent to present-day Council Tax) to public works designed primarily to alleviate unemployment. These ranged from simple things like the re-painting of railings on the recreation ground, which would take four men four weeks, and road repairs in Union Street which would cost about £100, of which £65 would be paid as wages, to far more ambitious projects such as a new electricity supply cable for London Road (£900, wages £150). Other projects, some attracting government grants and all carried out in the next year or two, included making hard courts for tennis in the city moat, to a new spate of council-house building which would add fresh lustre to the city's enviable record of slum clearance.

How successful all these measures were in combating unemployment is difficult to judge, but at least they must have been taken as proof that the Council was willing and able to do something about 'the unemployment problem'. One group of the unemployed even formed a deputation to meet the Mayor and discuss their plight with him. In the back of their minds, as already in mine, there must have been a conviction that this city was a self-governing entity, with real if admittedly limited powers.

No one could doubt that Canterbury was a special kind of place. Frequently we saw the city arms and read the motto under it, *Ave Mater Angliæ*, which Miss Pierce translated for us as 'Hail, Mother of England' – though without adding that it was the invention of an Edwardian Mayor. Although we would not have found it easy to say exactly that the letters CCBC stood for 'City and County Borough of Canterbury', we knew they meant that our city was something out of the ordinary. And so it was, for as a legacy from its history, Canterbury was the smallest County

Borough in the country, with wider powers of self-government than many a much larger place.

I have called the Council the 'hidden hand', and that was how I envisaged it until I reached the age of ten or eleven. Then, quite suddenly, I was able to see it at work, not yet in the flesh, but through the pages of the local newspapers. The monthly meetings of the Council regularly occupied nearly the whole of a large, seven-column page and ran to 6,000 or 7,000 words. Particularly interesting exchanges were quoted verbatim, so that a regular reader quickly got to recognize the oratorical style of the main pro-tagonists. Even the speakers' hesitations and repetitions, the pert questions of self-important newcomers and the Mayor's deft put-downs in response, were all faithfully recorded month by month.

These debates all took place in the Guildhall, an historic struc-ture that dated back to the seventeenth century and was already

The decaying sixteenth-century Guildhall was home to council meetings and the magistrates' court. It was damaged beyond repair by Second World War bombing then demolished amid a storm of public protest

in such a state of decay that members of the public, for whom accommodation was very limited, were able to overhear its proceedings, or those of the magistrates' court that also sat there (with the Mayor as chief magistrate throughout his year of office), in Currys' electrical shop next door. Eventually, with much heart-searching and amid a storm of protest, the Council agreed to its demolition in the 1950s in the belief – buttressed by much expert advice – that it was beyond repair.

The many who drank in the Council's debates had, however, no need to seek one of the limited spaces in the public gallery, or even to visit Currys, for they could find everything they needed in prodigious detail in the *Kentish Gazette* and its rivals. Each report of the monthly meeting of the Full Council began with a list of the aldermen and councillors present and those absent. The details of the Council officers in attendance left no doubt that here was the assembly of a city-state, tiny yet potent, in full charge of a wide range of powers. Among these officers were the Chief of Police and the Director of Education, and many another whose titles signifying real local authority have long since vanished; and yet others with titles that gave little hint of their widespread responsibilities. The Town Clerk, for instance, was in charge of the system of welfare, including the Workhouse at Nunnery Fields.

The debates can be described in a single word: theatre. The old Theatre Royal had been on the opposite side of Guildhall Street, a stucco-fronted building facing the flank of the stucco-encased Guildhall; but of the two, the latter must have had the larger and more faithful audience, thanks to the group of reporters busily using their perfect Pitman. The two 'stars' of its sessions were undoubtedly Alderman Barrett and Councillor Stone. This is clear enough from the press reports, and it was fascinatingly confirmed for me some twenty years ago when I talked to an old man who in his youth had worked in Barretts' accounts department. He told me how eagerly Barrett looked forward to the Full Council meetings. As he set off for one of them, he said to his office staff, 'Just you look at next Friday's *Gazette*. I've got it in for

Stone.' I like to think that this was when he knew that the promotion of Canterbury as a tourist centre was going to be one of the major topics of debate. It produced a notable clash between these two Titans, both men of humble origin with strongly contrasting characters and outlooks.

Stone was a tailor who, according to my grandfather, had had to work in the orchards as a bird-scarer in his younger days, but in adult life had become a recognized authority on the Poor Law. He began the debate on tourism by inveighing against the idea that ratepayers' money should be spent on advertising Canterbury:

There was no need to advertise Canterbury, he believed. Canterbury should be proud and content to enjoy that quiet dignity and those splendid traditions that were much cherished. He was still a believer in the old adage that 'good wine needs no bush'. It might be necessary, he argued, for some places to be advertised, but there was less reason for Canterbury to be advertised. It was advertised by Chaucer, and, long before Chaucer, by St Augustine. Those were the advertisements that appealed to the people whom they wanted to attract. (Hear, Hear.)

What Stone preached he also practised, for the windows of his modest tailor's shop in Palace Street, a few yards from Miss Pierce's school, contained just a few bolts of cloth, while on the fascia there was simply Stone's not very legible signature reproduced in gold leaf on a dark-green background. Prospective customers either knew already, or had to deduce for themselves, the nature of Stone's business.

To Alderman Barrett, a brilliant entrepreneur who had started life as a cycle repairer and whose Midas touch had led him to become the main local agent for Ford and then Rover cars, and master of one of the city's most obviously thriving businesses, Stone's thesis was anathema. 'Their friend Councillor Stone,' he said, 'would like to see the streets, possibly, overgrown with grass, with carts and donkeys being driven up the streets [Laughter].'

From that point, the contest descended into personalities, mere slapstick of much the same sort as occurred in a debate three years later:

Alderman Barrett: (referring to Councillor Stone): There is a man who has not put on a pair of gloves in his life.

Councillor Stone: Oh, haven't I? I did so long before you. I would not mind standing up to you now [Laughter].

Alderman Barrett: If, as a lad, you had gone to a gymnasium and had a proper lesson, you would never make the suggestion you have. Your own remarks prove you know nothing of boxing.

Councillor Stone: I was looking at it from an academic and philosophical point of view, and I knew that would be beyond you. There would be no boxing if there were no prizes. It is the acquisition of power in basic nature, wanting something for nothing.

Terribly feeble stuff, but at least it drew some to search out the 'good bits' who would otherwise have turned straight to the market reports from London, which gave the current prices for every kind of agricultural and horticultural crop. Others, finding the exchange of personalities distasteful, could move quickly on to more humdrum matters. They would learn perhaps that a new chief engineer had been engaged by the Council to run its electricity works in Northgate at a salary of £650 a year plus a bonus geared to the increase in consumption of units, or that a new librarian had been appointed at £350 (a bargain, this, for the modest young Lancastrian they took on, Frank Higenbottam, turned out to be not only a splendid librarian but also a remarkable intellect, capable of mastering outmoded kinds of shorthand and of writing a 'Teach Yourself' book, *Learning Russian by*

Reading, even though he never set foot in Russia). Or they might immerse themselves in the difficulties that had arisen in computing the Sanitary Inspector's travelling expenses when he exchanged his motor bicycle for a car. Much of this detail was trivial, but it did serve to give any attentive reader a sense of participating in the government of his city, and it often threw light on the widespread expertise the Council had at its command. Such a reader would soon get a pretty good idea of where the boundaries of the city's authority lay – that, for instance elementary education was a 'City' affair, but secondary education was shared with the County Council.

In this and other ways the local newspapers were primers of citizenship. Whenever the Council began to use new powers entrusted to it by central government, it had to face the question of how the public would react. One controversial issue of the 1930s was that of town planning. The idea that the design of private houses, and even such details as the addition of a garage, should be subject to the Council's approval, was still seen as something of an unwelcome novelty. In their local papers of around 1930, readers found what they needed to enable them to think about this question in – almost literally – concrete terms. The middle-class readers who enjoyed the clean air of the heights of South Canterbury found themselves faced with the awful prospect of a new lime-burning works in their vicinity, which would bring the threat of pollution right to their windows. In the ensuing Council debates, Alderman Barrett urged that the development should go ahead in view of its benefit to the local economy, even though this would mean overriding the designation in the Town Plan of South Canterbury as a residential area.

Here was an issue that aroused intense emotion among the most articulate section of the community. The workers in Abbots Mill, who lived in Mill Lane and other parts of the city centre, suffered pollution daily of a kind probably far worse than anything the new lime kiln would produce, but they accepted it quietly as the price of employment. Not so, the burghers of South Canterbury. They accosted councillors in the main street, and the Mayor, the Revd S. Gordon Wilson, quickly saw the need to enlighten the Council, in the knowledge that his message would be transmitted to all the interested parties through the local press:

> The Town Planning Committee was not a popular committee of the Council, and he thought very few members really knew much about its work. But the whole health of the country, which was getting more and more crowded, depended on town planning. It should be one of the most important committees of the whole Council.

This set the tone for the ensuing debate, which led the Council to turn down the lime works project. Among those offering evidence were the Cathedral architect, W. D. Caroe, who said that there had been more decay to the Cathedral fabric from pollution in the previous thirty years than in the preceding 300, and the Medical Officer of Health, Dr Harrison, who asked, 'If that had been the effect of pollution on stone, what must it be on children's lungs?' It isn't claiming too much, therefore, to suggest that one page of the *Kentish Gazette* in January 1930 may have achieved the difficult task of sowing two new ideas in the minds of many Canterbury citizens – that pollution was a problem to be grappled with, and that Town Planning (by then no novelty, for the city had had its first Town Plan as far back as 1922, and was just on the verge of getting its third) might really be quite a good idea.

Who were these aldermen and councillors, and what was their motivation? They were sometimes referred to as 'City Fathers', and that is an apt term, for their rule was decidedly paternalistic. They stood as individuals, only gradually and reluctantly adopting party labels, as during the course of the 1930s. In 1930, for instance, the campaign slogan of Alfred Baynton, the secretary of the East Kent Road Car Company who was later to become Mayor, was 'Baynton and Business Methods'. Catherine Williamson, the first woman to be Mayor

of Canterbury, recalled in the late 1940s the period leading up
to her installation in 1938:

> It would be difficult to describe Local Government in
> Canterbury from a political aspect in 1935. It might be said
> the general trend of thought was a sound Conservative one;
> on the other hand, politics did not enter very largely into the
> arena, and when a new member was chosen he or she was
> chosen I think more for their capacity to work in the interests
> of others than from a political standpoint. After a march of
> years the political point of view became more acute until
> today [1946] we have a wide gulf fixed between a section of
> thought on the Right and a section on the Left.

She went on to say that she thought this new state of affairs was
a good thing – but tantalizingly she gave no reasons why she felt
that if the relative absence of party labels had been a good thing in
the 1930s, it should not have continued to be so in the 1940s and
1950s. Even she could hardly have foreseen that a time would come
when local Councils and their elections would be regarded as
merely referendums on national policies rather than local issues.

Through the monthly press reports of its full meetings, followed by those of committees, the Council's activities were
brought home to all who had any concern about how the city was
run. There were moments, too, when we saw the Council not
merely through the long, cramped columns of the local newspapers, but in procession or on display. This might be when they
went annually to the Westgate Tower, the finest medieval town
gate in the country, to commemorate the death of its builder, Archbishop Sudbury, who was murdered in the Peasants' Revolt in
1381. Or it might be the Christmas service in the Cathedral, when
they filed in (not without some jostling for precedence, as my
friend William Urry described to me in the early post-war days),
led by the Town Sergeant bearing the mace, the aldermen robed
in scarlet and the councillors in blue, all with cocked hats of

antique design – albeit of much less antique provenance. But of all such civic occasions there was one whose true significance becomes apparent only when it is considered in hindsight.

This was the opening ceremony of the widened Broad Street in the summer of 1931, which has already been briefly mentioned in these pages but deserves a second look. A labour of months preceded it. Along with my school friends, I watched as the Star Brewery in Broad Street was demolished and gradually a magnificent stretch of the city wall, hidden for generations, was revealed. The adhering plaster of the old construction was picked away from the flint, but parts of it remain to this day in places where it would have been too destructive to remove. Then began the most exciting part of all – the formation of a fine, wide road constructed in a wholly novel way, by casting hexagonal sections of concrete that eventually were covered with tarmac, in place of the narrow lane that had belied the ancient name of Broad Street. The City Engineer explained and justified his unorthodox method to his professional institution, laying particular stress on the difficult sub-surface conditions, but we young onlookers knew nothing of these niceties. Sufficient for us was the thrill of seeing the mixing and pouring, the steel reinforcement, and all the other features of a technique that was then still very unfamiliar – and that in fact was to prove its worth for seventy years, with immensely heavier traffic than anyone ever conceived, before the fabric of the road had to be renewed. Flanking the new road, along the base of the newly revealed walls, the city's first purpose-built car park was constructed, equipped at the Burgate end with public lavatories which, for many years, were regarded as the finest in Kent – fit rivals even to the splendid facilities of the seaside towns, with wrought iron at the entrances to the two stairways and religiously burnished brass below.

In June there came the day of celebration of all this activity that had been the fruit of constant communication between the Council officers and their masters in Whitehall: a dais was erected along the city wall, just in front of the Queningate entrance to the

Cathedral precincts. Here the Council and all its officers, including even the registrar, Harry Houlden, whose signature graces my birth certificate, ensconced themselves. Before them there was an immense crowd, including a horde of schoolchildren who had all been assigned places marked out on the new roadway – to my bitter disappointment, I was not one of them. There were even some people perched on the rooftops of Broad Street. The robed Cathedral choir and clergy (though with no Dean, for Hewlett Johnson had not yet arrived) filed in through the Queningate, led by the cross-bearer and singing a hymn, and then the Salvation Army band struck up most appropriately 'All people that on Earth do dwell'.

Given such a preparation, no Mayor could have resisted the temptation to orate, and the Revd S. Gordon Wilson did not resist. He affirmed his belief that the British Empire was destined, under the providence of God, to lead the nations in the paths of plenteousness and peace. Then he turned to greet the guest of the day, Mr George Lansbury, the Commissioner for Public Works, who, he said, 'at great personal inconvenience had left a meeting of the Cabinet in order to be with them'.

Lansbury, too, had a vision of the future to impart, and it was a very different one to that of the Mayor. He had little to say about the few hundred yards of new road, but instead talked directly to the numerous schoolchildren. He commended the Council for its clearance of slum areas and for having spent some £600,000 on public housing. 'The day will come,' he said, 'in the lifetime of you boys and girls when you will have cleared away every unfit home in Canterbury.'

His praise was well directed. Only a short distance from where Lansbury spoke, there was an area of Northgate where shoddy housing had been hastily run up during the Napoleonic Wars. Here, in 1931, in a decaying two-up and two-down house with no bathroom or inside lavatory, lived a nine-year-old boy, with his mother and stepfather, who 'won the scholarship' two years later and became one of my schoolfellows. I knew him as Laker, F. A., but by the time he revisited the site of his birthplace and boyhood home in New Ruttington Lane, he had become Sir Freddie Laker and a millionaire. By then, thanks to slum clearance programmes before and after the war, that part of Northgate had been totally redeveloped. There was nothing of the old days to show his American wife, but he told her, 'No one should live like we did.'

For those with just a little money, new houses were going up on the outskirts at attractive prices: some that today fetch around £300,000 were for sale at £750, with only £25 asked as the deposit. But the city-centre poor, only 27 per cent of whom had bathrooms, needed something quite different: houses to rent at three-and-sixpence a week, a reasonable fraction of the weekly income which in many homes amounted to only £2 or £3 if the head of the household had a job. In parliamentary elections, the councillors were no doubt, as Catherine Williamson said, largely Conservative, though there were some – such as Hooker – who let slip the fact that they were Liberals. Labour supporters were a small minority on the Council; early in the 1930s Sidney Palmer, a prosperous fruit grower whose son Maurice was one of my schoolfellows, was to my knowledge the only one. How did it come about, then, that Councils of the 1920s and 1930s, consisting mainly of Right-leaning tradesmen, conceived and carried through a policy of re-housing the poor with a zeal that won Lansbury's commendation?

This policy was not without its critics. I often heard people say, 'Give these people a bathroom and they'll only put coal in the bath.' This was literally true, but quite untrue in its implications. The portable galvanized iron bath that came indoors for bath nights was often transported to the new council estates to serve as a coal bunker and feed the doubts of those who considered the working classes to be by nature feckless. Swimming at times against a strong current of local opinion, the Councils of the 1920s and 1930s managed to endow the city with well-planned estates whose tenants my father rightly saw as potential customers for his household fuels, whether destined for bath or bunker. The nettle bed at Thanington into which I dumped a wad of his advertisement leaflets has long gone, but the shame of that dereliction of duty still remains after nearly eighty years.

Two main reasons seem to account for this apparently improbable emphasis on building council houses. There was a genuine and widespread pride in the city, and it was seen as natural for the more prosperous to contribute to the general good. This was no new phenomenon. An eighteenth- and early-nineteenth-century tycoon, Simmons, after making a fortune from patent medicines, newspapers (including the *Kentish Gazette*) and flour milling (as owner of King's Mill, which burned down in 1933), converted the unkempt area of Dane John into a public park at great expense. Dr Beaney's questionable fortune enabled him to give his birthplace the public library and museum, still called by many 'the Beaney', while the artist Sidney Cooper not only provided the school of art that bore his name, but taught there himself without fee.

In the twentieth century, this tradition of 'munificence' continued. Charles Lefevre gave the Langton schools a pair of wrought-iron gates in the 1930s, which were last seen on a council dump fifteen or twenty years later; Frank Hooker's gift of Larkey Valley Woods was only one of his bequests to the city. To mark the Jubilee of King George V, Babs Hill was bought by public subscription in 1936 (my friend William Urry told me how he had contributed ten shillings, a large sum for him in those days); and most striking of all was the donation in 1936 by the Williamson family of Tower House, now the headquarters of the Lord Mayor, together with its vast and beautiful garden bordering the River Stour which is one of the city's main amenities – a gift that was capped by Stanley Jennings when he gave the fine Regency railings at its entrance.

Yet local 'munificence' alone is not a sufficient explanation. Even in the most prosy debates of the Council, a note of genuine idealism is clear. The Christian Socialist movement of the nineteenth century, and similar developments in nonconformist (and espe-

cially Baptist) circles following it, were reinforced by polemics in
the twentieth century such as Hugh Redwood's *God in the Slums*
and *Broken Shards* by Harold Begbie, which were among the few
newly published titles that found their way to my parents' book-
shelves. All these trends encouraged the idea that, notwithstanding
the doubts of some about coal in bathtubs, religious faith ought to
be expressed by positive action to alleviate poverty, and in particular by providing decent housing. When Lansbury got up to speak
in Broad Street on that sunny day in June 1931, he knew that the
widening of an inner-city road was far less important to most of his
audience than the re-housing of the poor.

One question remains. This was a day of celebration – but of
what? To answer this, it is necessary to scrutinize afresh the guest
list. Its most curious feature is that those present included no
fewer than fourteen Mayors from Kent and one from Sussex – but
no county councillors. In essence, the celebration was for something much larger than the removal of the brewery, the revelation
of the wall, the making of a fine stretch of new road, or even the
creation of the best public lavatory in Kent. It was about the
power and majesty of local government, the ability of a local
Council to do great things, and to do them by speaking direct to
the mandarins in Whitehall, bypassing the upstart County
Council whose history went back only to the 1880s, not the thousand years or more of which the boroughs could boast. Sweltering
in their robes, the Mayors could find great reassurance on that day
in the continuing importance of local government.

And reassurance was something they all needed, for their role
and influence were clearly under threat. In Canterbury itself, the
last years of the 1930s would see the Council facing two great
challenges. One was the problem of Sunday cinemas, the resolution of which placed new limitations on the City Fathers'
traditionally paternalistic style of government. The other was
the need to prepare for war, a task in which the Council gave
notable proof of its continuing vitality and organizing power.
The *Daily Mail* ran a campaign deriding it for spending so much

on building up its capacity to deal with air raids, but in the ensuing war the city's state of preparedness was triumphantly vindicated.

'Small is beautiful' would have been a fitting motto for the Councils of the 1920s and 1930s, but it was not invented until the post-war period, when the decline of local government's powers and status was clear for all to see. Central government periodically declares its faith in local decision-making, but its actions show what it really thinks about local Councils: not 'small is beautiful', but 'small is negligible'.

9

Blean Was a Far Cry

WHEN THE WIND was right, 'Dicky' Jannells's stentorian voice could carry from an open-air meeting of the Salvation Army in Westgate Grove right to Blean, two miles away over the hill and dale. So my grandparents affirmed.

For all that, in my boyhood, Blean was truly rural, a world apart from Canterbury, its ways of life quite different from our ways. My mother told me that until the coming of Woods's Bus, that dark-brown, rumbling vehicle with solid tyres that I travelled on once or twice before pneumatically shod successors took over, almost the only way to get from her home at Blean Bottom

As a young boy, Ken would make the two-mile journey to Blean to visit his grandparents on the rumbling Whitstable bus

to Canterbury was to walk. The one alternative, and I cannot understand why she ever chose to use it, was to trudge a mile and a half to Blean Halt, a little shack on the single-track line from Whitstable to Canterbury that had functioned, after a fashion, since 1830.

When my grandparents set up home in Blean on their marriage in the 1890s, my grandfather scratched their moving-in date with a diamond on one of the kitchen window-panes. There in Brook Cottage (or in Number One, Brook Cottages – country people are content to leave such ambiguities unresolved) they lived for the rest of their lives, for most of the time in conditions of pre-Victorian simplicity, and only in their last years did their mode of life begin to take on a modern cast. Until about 1930, every drop of drinking water came from 'the spring', an ever-welling source, covered by a hinged flap, about five minutes' walk from their back door. Every day my grandfather had to shoulder the wooden yoke from which two pails were hung; and I learned at an early age that only one of the pails just inside the back door was of drinking water: the other, for washing and washing up, had been dipped from the rain water butt or even from the brook that ran (though sometimes dry in summer) alongside the house. There was no gas, no electricity; a small oil stove served to supplement the black coal-fired kitchen 'range' which heated both the room and the small oven, and for lights there were only oil lamps and candles.

At Brook Cottage and its semi-detached neighbouring cottage, in which my aunt, and two cousins, came to live after she was widowed early in the 1920s, almost every one of the domestic details pointed some contrast to our own city-dwelling ways. Perhaps the most striking difference of all was the sanitary arrangements: earth closets, in an outbuilding that also contained the wash-house, of which the contents were periodically removed through cupboard doors in the end wall of the outbuilding. No doubt the garden, easily an acre in extent, owed some of its remarkable fertility to this primitive method of sewage disposal. I

Ken's grandfather and grand-mother, with a friend, stand outside their tiny cottage in Blean. The cottage had no gas, electricity or mains drainage and water had to be fetched from a spring

am not sure that at first my grandmother even had a drain-way sink, for she used to tell in uproarious detail how she had flung her washing-up water from the back door towards the brook, just at the moment when the baker's roundsman arrived to receive it full in the face.

Then in the mid-1930s came change at last. The cottages fronted on to the main Canterbury–Whitstable road, and con-necting main services – first water, then electricity and gas – was relatively simple and cheap, especially as the electricity company offered a 'package deal' at a guaranteed price. This meant that the electric light was installed, together with one socket for radio in the kitchen, but the rest of the house remained in the oil-lit nineteenth century. Even in the kitchen the big brass oil lamp was often lit, because my grandmother found it less trying to her eyes than the electric light. So my memories of Grandma's home are in a rich chiaroscuro of dim light and deep shadows; the brass ornaments on her mantelpiece – a Lilliputian fireplace complete with coal bucket and fire-irons – glowing vividly, her cat almost invisible under the great armchair covered with a tasselled shawl, which the latest lot of kittens always found an irresistible plaything. Opposite the fireplace the wall was of tongued and grooved boarding into which were cut two doors with latches, one a pantry and the other opening on to a narrow stairway with a reflector-backed oil lamp, like a gleaming eye, fastened to the wall.

A steep step divided the kitchen from the front room, for the cottages were built on the ground that sloped sharply down from front to back. By day in that room, there was nearly always an atmosphere of subdued sunlight, whatever the weather, for the cream-coloured blinds were usually half drawn to keep the sun off the ugly 1890s suite of two armchairs and a sofa. It was a little-used room, reserved mostly for Sundays and Christmas. The house door led into it from the front, but it was hardly ever opened: some time in the distant past it had 'stuck', and no one seemed to feel there was much point in unsticking it. To me, the most fascinating item of its contents was a watercolour, by some Canadian relation, of a child interrogating a dog. Or was it the dog who was putting the questions? I liked, too, to look in the elaborately bound photograph album, full mostly of departed faces whose identities did not stay in my memory from one opening to the next. A yellow-toothed piano that was rarely played and a cabinet gramophone used only as a pedestal for some of Grandma's household goods took up much of the remaining space round the central table; but stowed in a cupboard were a few hidden treasures – an old teaset for very special occasions, a violin in a magnificent leather case that my grandfather had made (was it in the hope that one of his three daughters would learn to play it?), and a superannuated Edison Standard phonograph with two purpose-made cases to hold its cylindrical records. On one of these records, broken but still playable after nearly eighty years, I can hear my father and my grandmother singing a duet, for this machine was able to record as well as play.

It was upstairs in the back bedroom that the essence of that home seemed to exist in an especially concentrated form. From the voluminous depths of the feather bed I could see, on top of a chest of drawers, a fascinating toy: a beautifully made and painted model of a ship on a stormy sea, covered by a glass dome of which part was painted to form the background. Years ago, I was told, this model could be put into action: the boat would toss on the waves while a tune came from within. On the wall behind it was the large framed picture inspired by *Pilgrim's Progress*, which portrayed the danger of deviating from the path of righteousness.

It was not the piety of this picture that made it seem so profoundly representative of that home in Blean, but rather its archaic and other-worldly flavour, so perfectly in keeping with the fact that the steep steps up to Grandma's back door led to an interior that belonged to half a century earlier, and that lying in the long grass of the 'slip' where ancient trees blossomed and fruited almost unvisited throughout the year, I was neighbour to the ant and grasshopper and to no human being whatever. This quality of remoteness runs like a red thread through every part of my childhood memories of Blean. It was not then a village-suburb of Canterbury just beyond the university. It was 'the country', where you walked from home with your cousins to the village church all the way by footpaths leading through crowsfoot-speckled meadows; where to get your milk you went up the hill to the farm near the top, waiting while the wise-cracking young farm worker ran a few gallons over the cooler; where the houses scattered along the stretch of road spanning the valley were served by a post office – pint-sized in a little cottage where my mother's friend, Nessie Holttum, was postmistress, by a general store almost opposite my grandparents' house and by a forge, and the Hare and Hounds pub nearly facing each other as the road began to rise towards Whitstable. So provided, my grandparents must have felt that travelling to Canterbury on foot or, later, by bus was a matter of choice rather than necessity.

Then, as now, there were almost two Bleans. There was my grandparents' part, Blean Bottom and its environs, fringed by what remained of the 'Forest of the Blee' as Chaucer called it. And there was the somewhat more populous settlement nearer to Whitstable but off the main road, around the vicarage and the school and fairly close to the church that stood then, as it still does, amid open fields. So sequestered, the church of St Cosmas and St Damian was not the most conspicuous of the village's buildings: that role fell to the magnificent cow-house built by Albert Price on the strength of the farming profits he made in the First World War, a handsome edifice of sturdy brick with a clock tower, which the Prince of Wales was persuaded to declare open – an arrangement that was cancelled later in the day with very little explanation. The building has gone, but the clock tower has been remembered in a small shopping centre on its site.

Blean is therefore disjointed and puzzling; and much the same might be said of my grandfather's life history. A group of local historians is now bringing sense to Blean's topographical oddities, showing for instance that a long-forgotten village once clustered round the church. I wish I could do the same with the fragments that I know of my grandfather's life, which are so difficult to fit into a logical pattern.

This is equally true of its religious and its secular aspects. He was at some time churchwarden of the parish church; yet my mother told me how, when she was at the village school, the vicar railed at her for being a Salvationist, and at other children for attending the Methodist chapel that had recently established itself. I find similar problems in piecing together the details of Grandad's working life. He was the village postman, working long hours for exceedingly modest pay and covering a wide area stretching to Denstroude and beyond. Yet at the same time, it seems, he was a 'cycle agent': that is, he assembled cycles from parts supplied by the manufacturers, selling the completed machines and also others that he renovated. A memoir by a Blean resident who died a few years ago records how, in his youth, he bought a secondhand bicycle from 'Mr Wood at Blean Bottom' for ten shillings, which he was allowed to pay off at a shilling a week. My grandfather used to tell me how he had been a cycling enthusiast from his early youth, riding the pedal-less 'boneshaker' kind of machine, and then penny-farthings, until the modern 'safety bicycle' came on the market.

This was the moment to act. He built a series of well-made sheds which gradually extended along the brook-side behind the cottage, and there in his scanty spare time he plied his trade of assembling, renovating and repairing. It was a time when the potential of cycling seemed almost endless: in one of his pre-1914 visions of the future, H. G. Wells envisaged workers cycling to their factories on multi-seat machines.

By the early 1930s, when the final phase of my grandfather's working life began, his days as a postman were far behind him, and

Ken's maternal grandfather, Tom Wood, was the village postman, but he found time to develop a profitable side-line in repairing and constructing bicycles just when cycling was becoming popular

the cycle business no longer had a place for solitary rural craftsmen working to assemble machines from parts. Instead, he had a tiny workshop in Oaten Hill, on the corner of Cossington Road, where he mended boots and shoes and occasionally made them to measure using bought-in 'uppers': assembly and adaptation were second nature to him. An old and grey-haired man then, he cycled from Blean and back again each day on a racing-type machine with dropped handlebars; and in his shop I would find him, delighted to talk as soon as he had taken the brads out of his mouth, whenever I took in my shoes to have them re-soled with 'Dri-Ped' or fitted with Blakeys' Boot Protectors.

This ceaseless industry did not go unrewarded. By the mid-1920s he owned both of Brook Cottages and other property in Canterbury. Long before that, he sent my mother to school at the Simon Langton, but she was not particularly happy there and perhaps that is why her sisters did not follow her. It was not easy, anyway, to improve on what the village school alone could offer at that time. My mother's youngest sister, Hilda, wrote in a beautifully formed hand and spelt better than many present-day undergraduates. She became a prized member of the staff of Mr T. H. Sayers, who ran a sewing machine shop in Burgate and was secretary of the Chamber of Trade. All her schooling must have ceased at fourteen – though it was clear from what Mr Sayers said of her that she must have continued to educate herself 'on the job'.

Then, in about 1925, his family 'off his hands', my grandfather made one of his biggest decisions – to buy a car, a Singer open tourer costing some £250, which was as much as some working men earned in a year. Cars were still very much luxury items. This one was a tinny little affair whose wheels – like flat dinner plates with four nuts protruding at the centre – typified the basic crudeness of its manufacture. He built a garage for it in a field opposite the cottage, but he never drove it. Just as my father could never make the leap from the age of the horse to that of the car, so my grandfather, for all his addiction to technical change, was never quite able to climb out of his nineteenth-century rut.

The ultimate stage of his working life, before he spent a few, final years completely at leisure, came after an accident put an end to his cycling. Then he came full circle, back to his sheds where for three or four years he continued his cobbling at a large westward-facing window a few paces from his back door. The rhythmic tapping of his hammer mingled with the rushing of water in the brook, while behind him stretched his unused but still serviceable range of sheds, a few forgotten tools rusting on the benches, the vices' jaws gaping, ancient acetylene lamps and other relics cob-webbed on high shelves, and only the spiders at work in these abandoned arcades of industry.

Chaucer well knew, and probably the medieval world at large knew with him, that death often comes by stealth. How I might have questioned my grandfather about his past life, if I had ever thought seriously about the possibility of his no longer being there. But such foresight is rarely given to the young; so when I said farewell to him in the windswept churchyard at Blean in 1941, there were only a few images that I could treasure from conversa-tions with him – how as a boy of ten he had heard in Blean a distant rumble, as of thunder but continuous: the guns of the Franco-Prussian War of 1870; and how the first bicycles had sent up clouds of white dust from the chalky surfaces of the then untarred roads. But how he had come by his remarkable skill as leatherworker and mechanic, and a hundred other questions I would have liked to put to him, I did not know and never shall.

With my grandmother I showed a little more sense, though not enough. Somehow I spent a few days with her not long after my grandfather's death. Until then I had been somewhat afraid of her, for although she could be vastly entertaining to a young child – especially when she ventured into one of her marvellous imitations of a Punch and Judy show – she was large, com-manding, utterly fearless and outspoken. Many of her stories were of devastating ripostes that she had uttered, of incidents (such as the drenching of the baker's man) that would have been embarrassing to almost anyone else, but that to her were merely laughable. We had never before been very close companions, but now we were.

She was no longer reading anything, other than the occasional letter or message which she managed with the help of a magnifying glass, but that did not matter because instead she had the radio. So after supper we tuned in to one of her favourite comedy programmes. She knew them all. Rob Wilton, with his famous monologue beginning 'The day war broke out', was held in high esteem. He and other radio comics seemed to me to belong to the tradition of Billy Williams, of whom I had a box of a dozen cylindrical records stowed in my bedroom cupboard which I occasionally played on our long-horned Edison phonograph. But what really captivated my grandmother was Tommy Handley's *Itma*, a completely new style of radio comedy programme, full of catch-phrases that had already become part of her language alongside the older phrases from Dickens and from family myth. 'Barkis is willing', she would often say rather than a plain 'Yes'; and in family gatherings there would be a spontaneous cry of laughter all round whenever she or Grandad uttered the words 'fat as a mole' or 'he's only 'leven'. How the first of these originated no one could really explain, but the other dated from the time when Grandad and a friend presented themselves at the half-price gate of the Crystal Palace, meeting the objection that one of them *must* be over fourteen. Now, thanks to Tommy Handley, his scriptwriters and her continually used wireless set, Grandma could indulge to the full her long-nurtured propensity for catch-phrases: 'Can I do you now, sir?' 'After you, Claude.' 'No, after you, Cecil' – and half a dozen others that passed not only into her language, but for a time into the nation's as well.

The radio switched off, she would start to reminisce. One of her stories was of O. Sequah, a quack doctor who visited the city around the 1880s. His name had an American flavour, and certainly his doctoring owed something to the methods of hot gospellers. He hired the Agricultural Hall in Rhodaus Town, opposite the city wall, which later became the premises of the

Canterbury Motor Company. Here his audiences were able to see immediate and spectacular results from his treatment – the crippled throwing away their crutches, and so forth. One of his specialities, Grandma said, was the swift and allegedly painless extraction of teeth – with no anaesthetic, but accompanied by a brass band that played extra loudly at the crucial moments.

The wind of change – stronger by far than any that bore Dicky Jannells's voice over the chasm between city and village – has swept through Blean in the half-century since Grandad died and the forty years since Grandma followed him to that tempestuous graveyard. No longer is there a Nessie Holttum hand-stamping every outgoing letter 'Blean', for it and all the other surrounding villages are part of Canterbury now. New building has gone on apace, giving the village something of a suburban flavour. Are Blean's people, then, losing – or have they already lost – all sense of being village dwellers?

Happily the answer seems to be 'No'. Just as within the old city of Canterbury itself in recent years a host of locally based community associations have sprouted, so in most of the surrounding villages local societies flourish and local pride of place seems to be growing. Such pride cannot fail to be nurtured by the awakened interest in local history. In Blean, this movement has already produced and preserved at least one precious memoir of recent times, and has begun to reveal the village's – literally – buried medieval past. To this growing pile of knowledge and understanding I gratefully offer this little sketch of the life that my grandparents, richly endowed though equipped with few of what are now counted necessities, embarked on at the cottage by the brook over a century ago.